**Other Books by Robert L. Willett**

*One Day of the Civil War:*
*America in Conflict, April 10, 1863*

*The Lightning Mule Brigade:*
*Abel Streight's 1863 Raid into Alabama*

*Russian Sideshow: America's Undeclared War, 1918–1920*

*An Airline at War: Pan Am's China National Aviation*
*Corporation and Its Men*

# THE HUNT FOR JIMMIE BROWNE

# THE HUNT
# FOR JIMMIE
# BROWNE

## AN MIA PILOT IN WORLD WAR II CHINA

### ROBERT L. WILLETT

Potomac Books
*An imprint of the University of Nebraska Press*

All rights reserved. Potomac Books is an imprint of the
University of Nebraska Press.
Manufactured in the United States of America.

Photos courtesy of the author unless otherwise noted.

Library of Congress Cataloging-in-Publication Data
Names: Willett, Robert L., 1926– author.
Title: The hunt for Jimmie Browne: an MIA pilot in World War II
China / Robert L. Willett.
Description: [Lincoln]: Potomac Books, an imprint of the
University of Nebraska Press, [2020] | Includes bibliographical
references and index.
Identifiers: LCCN 2019015634
ISBN 9781640120259 (cloth: alk. paper)
ISBN 9781640122833 (epub)
ISBN 9781640122840 (mobi)
ISBN 9781640122857 (pdf)
Subjects: LCSH: Browne, James Sallee, 1921–1942. | Air
pilots—United States—Biography. | China National Aviation
Corporation—Employees—Biography. | World War, 1939–1945—
Missing in action—Biography. | World War, 1939–1945—
Casualties—China. | World War, 1939–1945—War work—China.
| China National Aviation Corporation—History—20th century.
| Aircraft accidents—China—History—20th century. | Aircraft
accidents—Investigation—China.
Classification: LCC TL540.B7444 .W55 2020 | DDC 940.54/8—
dc23 LC record available at https://lccn.loc.gov/2019015634

Set in Lyon Text by Mikala R. Kolander.

This book is dedicated to the crew of CNAC No. 60

John J. Dean

James S. Browne

K. L. Yang

Three men who saw the need to act even before others

# Contents

## Preface

This book is about our search for my cousin James Sallee Browne, copilot of a C-47 flown for China National Aviation Corporation (CNAC). The plane left Kunming, China, on November 17, 1942, destined for Dinjan, India, across the Himalayan Mountains on a high-risk route called the Hump. Their plane vanished, and for years there were no efforts to find the plane or its three-man crew.

The news that Jimmie was missing came from CNAC headquarters, then in Chungking, simply stating that his plane had not arrived at its destination and now was officially declared missing. Six months to the day later, the U.S. State Department declared him dead. He was twenty-one years old, newly engaged, and an only son. His parents never did recover.

It is hard to state an exact date when our family's search for Jimmie began, but the project has been with us, part time or full time, for over twenty-five years. For months we would add nothing to our basic few facts, but then we found others who could, and would, help. One of the two main players was Clayton Kuhles, president of MIA Recoveries, Inc. of Prescott, Arizona. The other was the China National Aviation Corporation Association. Their role was communicating, supporting, and, not to be overlooked, funding.

No organization exists in a vacuum, and CNAC was no exception. A number of organizations played major or minor roles in China's tragic war years, and Americans, even before Pearl Harbor, played significant parts in some of them. The American Volunteer Group (Flying Tigers) was by far the best known, but even before they organized, Claire Chennault was advising the fledgling Chinese Air Force and American volunteers were helping units, both air and ground, as China fought alone against the invading Japanese.

Chinese losses, military and civilian, during those early war years were great. And present throughout was the fledgling airline CNAC, whose success through eighteen years of war was a testimony to the early pioneers of aviation, many of whom paid for their adventure with their lives.

Jimmie was one of these.

## Acknowledgments

Any written work that covers several decades owes its existence to scores of people, organizations, repositories, and conversations, and I wish to thank all those with whom I have had dealings since this effort began. I can list only a few whose efforts were critical to the book.

First, to Clayton Kuhles and MIA Recoveries, Inc., I owe my greatest thanks. Clayton started with me back in 2004 and has been the principal source of information needed for the location of CNAC No. 60. It was Clayton who found the aircraft.

Second, Angie Chen, daughter of copilot Wei Ling Chen and fellow member of China National Aviation Corporation Association. It was Angie who found author Liu Xiatong and his book *Flying the Hump*, and later established contacts with Fan Jianchuan and Sun Chunlong.

Tom Moore is the creator of the website CNAC.org, which is a veritable encyclopedia of all things CNAC. Organizations such as University of Miami's Richter Library provided a wealth of information from its Pan American Airways collection. The Hoover Institute for War, Revolution and Peace on the Stanford University campus held collections of several noted CNAC and Chinese officials as well as data on the American Volunteer Group. My cousin Josh Rushton miraculously converted 1920s 16mm movies into crisp, clear videos. Helen Cole was an early supporter; we mourned her loss in 2018.

Most important to me during this project were my three off-spring: Tom was my travel companion and caregiver on four trips, Leslie was the computer expert and resource person, and Barb was my copyeditor, proofreader, and final manuscript compiler. Without these three I would still be struggling to comply with Abigail's requirements.

My Potomac editors who suffered through my delays, post-ponements, and my sometimes unorganized thought processes deserve accolades for their patience and compassion.

# THE HUNT FOR JIMMIE BROWNE

# PART 1

## JIM AND CHINA

# 1

## James Sallee "Jimmie" Browne

We lost Jimmie on November 17, 1942, although we had no news of that fact for probably a week. The war was almost a year old at the time, but it was before the casualty lists began to appear in the *Chicago Tribune* and other news sources, so his death was singularly difficult for us to accept.

Jim was twenty-one, two months short of his twenty-second birthday, and I, Jim's cousin, had just turned sixteen. I remember little about that time except the monumental sadness at the news. At first it was not sadness that he was dead but that he was "missing" on a flight from Kunming, China, to Dinjan, India. That meant there was hope, but that hope lasted only until June 16, 1943, when the U.S. State Department changed his classification to "presumed dead." That was a double whammy for his mom and dad, now without any hope.

The Brownes were a reasonably typical family, with a few exceptions. Jim was an only child, born on January 27, 1921, in Hinsdale, Illinois. He was adopted by the Brownes; his mother gave him up when he was just six months old. However, there was some uncertainty about the year of his birth. His 1940 Riverside Military Academy yearbook, the *Bayonet*, showed his birth date as January 27, 1922, and years later a ship's manifest from the *Leticia*, which brought Jim home from England on April 8, 1942, also showed the year 1922; however, most of his work records listed the year as 1921.

Trying to get birth information from official records was unsuccessful. Going through the Midwest Adoption Service in Chicago and even trying the adoption court in Cook County proved fruitless as adoption records are sealed and can be reopened only by petition of relatives closer than any that survive. Fortunately the Cook County Court did consent to give me a copy of the adoption approval; it blanked out Jim's name and other particulars but gave us the dates that were important.

Sadly, Harriet Browne, Jim's adopted mother, before her death had destroyed everything about Jimmie—photos, letters, memorabilia, and keepsakes—so little remains of his world. Whatever prompted her to erase her only child is a real mystery. However, all his work records with the British Overseas Airways Corporation, Air Transport Auxiliary, and China National Aviation Corporation show him to be born in 1921, a date that Jim may have supplied to bolster his credentials. When I received the Consent to Adoption, the matter was settled, the birth date confirmed as 1921.

The family thought that Jim was adopted at birth by his new parents, Harriet Sallee Browne, forty-one at the time, and Herbert Spencer Browne, forty-three. Christened James Sallee Browne, Jim was their first, and would be their only, child. However, the adoption paper indicated that Jim was actually born in Hinsdale, Illinois, a western Chicago suburb, and adoption was not finalized until June 8, 1921. The mother's name was blanked out on the Hinsdale form, but the form stated clearly that she relinquished any "claim of any character that [she] may have in the said child and consent to the adoption of said child by Herbert S. Browne and Harriet S. Browne."[1] Jim never got a birth certificate until January 1942, when he registered for the draft. His formal adoption papers did not quote a birth date, so his parents petitioned the court to establish January 27, 1921, as his date of birth, saying he needed the official date so he could get his birth certificate for "military purposes." That was even though he had been in England for seven months flying with the Royal Air Force Ferry Command.

The Brownes, being older than most new parents, over the years had problems coping with a son who was curious, adventuresome, and very active. There was plenty of affection, but as Jim grew,

JAMES SALLEE "JIMMIE" BROWNE

he tested the parental controls often. Even so, life was good for the Brownes at 653 Hill Road in affluent Winnetka, Illinois, as Jim began his schooling.

Harriet, always called "Hadda," was a wonderful person with a game leg that caused her to use a cane in her rather awkward walking. She was a serious lady, very much at home with household duties but uneasy in her social life on the few occasions when she ventured from the house. She doted on Jim, and he was very fond of her, but he rebelled often, especially when he wanted something that was not forthcoming. In later years he had everything he could have wanted: a new 1939 Buick convertible sedan, a motorcycle, and all the flying hours he could fit in. I think it was easier to give in to Jim than to fight him. But he remained a likeable, personable boy and young man, even though he was spoiled. He treated his parents with affection and respect, and family members who remember him said that he was really a joy to have around.

Mothers during World War II had a particularly difficult time as they prepared to send their children off to unknown dangers and the lure of battle. The magic date was a young man's eighteenth birthday, when he was required to register for the draft. After that, events moved swiftly toward induction, primarily into one of the three services: army, navy, or marines. While girls did not have to register for the draft, they too felt a pull toward war work, including the military, though combat was not a real possibility.

Herbert Browne was never called anything but Brownie. Tall, slim, with a love of his pipe, he was quiet and comfortable in any group. He loved working, and in the shed in the back of the house he spent hours building and repairing all sorts of things out of wood. A visit to his shop was a treat, getting to smell the woods and leather. He and Jim were close and spent the early years on many outings with nearby family members. Movies of the two of them show Jim looking out from a swing, leaning on his dad's leg and seeming very content. Brownie was also a man of words. He worked at Rand McNally Company as a proofreader for textbooks and other publications. Cousin Helen Cole wrote that Rand McNally held him in such high regard that on his death, they paid his full commission on a contract that had never been signed. A very quiet man, he was puzzled at the energy and the adventure-some activities of his young son, but his love overcame the uneasy relationship. Brownie died in February 1952; Hadda lasted five more years and died in 1957.

Young men could enlist before their eighteenth birthday and so select their branch of service, and I remember that Dad and I had a real challenge trying to convince Mom to sign the necessary papers to enlist shortly after I turned seventeen. Hadda, being so close to Jimmie, must have had a really difficult time when he made his move to get in the war.

Even after going overseas, many a young man fabricated his whereabouts to keep the family from concern about his safety. When I was recalled to the Korean War in 1950, my mother was still recovering from a severe stroke, so I sent all my letters with a Japanese return address. I landed in Korea in January 1951, but it wasn't until May 7 that Mom learned the truth. It was not a particularly difficult dodge, and by May life on the Korean peninsula was far less exciting than it had been in the first quarter of the year.

When Jim went to Canada and then on to England, Hadda had no such protection from her knowledge of his dangerous work. Not only was he flying new and powerful aircraft in wartime conditions, but the presence of German planes on the scene made his job even riskier. There was no hiding that fact from Hadda, and it took its toll.

I know Brownie did his best to console Hadda, but there was only so much he could do to keep her from dwelling on her only son's dangerous life. Much is made about the wartime contributions of people such as Rosie the Riveter and those who manned the nation's defenses and its production, but the agonies suffered by helpless mothers as they watched their precious sons march into the cauldrons of war is certainly worthy of praise and respect. Hadda paid an awful price for Jim's enthusiastic participation in the war.

Jimmie had other family in Winnetka. Hadda's niece Josephine (Dodie) lived in nearby Glencoe with her husband, Tom, and daughters, Sallee and Susan, and their older brother, Harry. Tom was Thomas Pope Mehlhop, my mother's brother and a World War

I vet who served with the fledgling U.S. Army Air Service, flying their vintage aircraft. Tom was to report to a frontline squadron the day the armistice was signed in November 1918.

Hadda and Dodie were close to the same age, making Jim Dodie's first cousin, although they were some thirty years apart. There was some mixing with the two families, but Tom and Dodie were gregarious and outgoing, while Hadda and Brownie were more reclusive by nature. Still, there was a loving relationship with the noisier Mehlhop family that kept them in close touch.

My family mixed frequently with Tom and Dodie but not so much with Hadda and Brownie. My dad, Robert Willett, my mom, Katherine, my sister, Louise (Wease), and I lived not far from Jim, but as we were growing up he was only a blip on our horizon. The five years that separated us in age was a great hurdle in the teen years. But I heard about his exploits, and as he grew older, taller, and better looking, I began to long for his qualities, mixed in with some envy.

Occasionally Tom and Dodie would host both families during a holiday season, and my memories of Jim from those times are the most vivid. It seemed to me that he grew more than a foot each time we met, but it is recorded that he topped out at six foot one, a giant next to my max of five six.

We all attended New Trier Township High School in Winnetka. Jim was the first to start. The Brownes lived close to the school, so initially he rode his bike, but soon he had a motorcycle, to the admiration of all. How he persuaded Hadda to let him get such a machine is a wonder, particularly since he was not much of a student.

I never heard details of his antics, but when Jim was completing his freshman year at New Trier High School, the Brownes thought he needed a heavier hand and enrolled him at Howe Military Academy in Howe, Indiana. I remember him coming home in his Howe uniform, probably in 1938, showing off to his old friends and to a few of us who were neighbors. The uniform always seemed to look just right on him and exaggerate his good looks. But even Howe was not able to bring out his best as a student, so next he was sent to Riverside Military Academy in Gainesville, Georgia. There he found his calling in aviation.

Hadda and Brownie watched his high school progress with great concern, hoping his Cs and Ds would turn to As and Bs. Aviation was his only passion, and it showed in his last year at Riverside. When he was home for short vacations, Hadda and Brownie gloried in his popularity with the Winnetka young ones, particularly the girls, and were deeply saddened at every departure.

Riverside Military Academy has been educating young boys since 1907 and has a great reputation. Boys in grades seven to twelve are housed in the sprawling 206-acre campus dominated by the school's fortress-like buildings. Today Riverside has an enrollment of 530 boys who are housed in spartan rooms but enjoy all the benefits of a first-class preparatory school. The rolling hills of Gainesville give a dramatic setting for the school, and this is where Jim fell in love with flying. Even in those days Riverside had an aviation course which included private pilot preparation and, according to Jim's Riverside transcript, a multi-engine rating. Besides his fascination with flying, little else seemed to interest him in the academic world. His grades were average or a little lower.

At Riverside, although aviation was available it was not a real part of the curriculum, being treated more or less like an elective, and it did substitute for some athletics. The program began when the school originated a ground school for those interested in moving on to the Army Air Corps. Gradually flight lessons were added and cadets could earn their private pilot's license as well as getting additional hours in bigger models than the trainers. A *Miami Herald* article dated March 3, 1940, gave considerable information about the program. Led by Capt. George L. Rutherford, the program enrolled thirty-five students. The Academy was founded in Georgia and established a seasonal campus in Hollywood, Florida, in the early 1930s; flight training was done mostly at Miami's Municipal Airport. Since its beginning there had been no accidents, a great record. The *Herald* article published photos of cadets and instructors at radio sets, tackling engines, and student James Hand just completing his first solo flight. Best of all is a fairly large photo of fifteen of the cadets, with Jimmie grim-faced and erect. It is one of the few photos of him that has survived.[2] The reporter noted that the aviation class in 1937 actually built an airplane on the campus, so the program that Jim found in 1939–40 was well established.

To balance things, a naval preparatory class was taught by Lt. M. F. Eddy, a navy pilot, although the subject appeared to be related more to naval seamanship than aviation.

Both at school and at home, Jim made friends easily. One of his Riverside classmates was Franklin Johnson from Wilmette. Frank too was interested in flying, but he was not in the aviation course at Riverside. Yet, because they came from the same neighborhood, they became friends both at school and at home. Frank remembers Jim well; they double-dated on occasion in Chicago, and he recalled Jim's new 1939 Buick convertible sedan that they used on at least one date. "Jim was always looking for excitement and frequently pushed the envelope too far and had to be reined in."

With a bit of a wild streak Jim did not always conform to his parents' expectations. They lavished toys and later cars and motorcycles on him to try to keep him on course, but he found others of his age and hung out with them. His academic work was never what could be called exceptional, except in aviation.

That seemed to be the case for some other North Shore friends as well; Bob Ross and Andy Price often joined Jim in pranks. One episode that Frank remembered was when Jim, Bob, and Andy took Jim's new car and drove it onto the fairway of a local golf course, spinning wheelies to leave as their calling cards. Frank doesn't remember the end of that story, but I think it was one of Jim's more serious run-ins with the local officials. Frank never mentioned it, but I think he might have been part of that escapade as well.

Jim settled into his one year at Gainesville in the fall of 1939, and as evidenced by his transcript, he still had some discipline problems. A cryptic notation on his transcript reported that he had been Absent Without Leave on November 3, 1939. Further, the transcript stated he had been given a Military Efficiency Medal, also in November, but that medal was revoked in April 1940 and a promotion to corporal in October 1939 was reversed in April, when he was reduced to private.

On the good side was the fact that he had earned his private pilot's license as well as his multi-engine rating. So when he graduated from Riverside on June 3, 1940, he was ready for a flying job; college had hardly been discussed. In the 1940 *Bayonet* yearbook Jim's future was to include Harvard, but I think that might have been inserted with tongue in cheek.

After graduation the Brownes were happy to have him home but saw little of him as he gained more flying time and stirred up the neighborhood with his motorcycle and his beautiful new Buick convertible. He also apparently became serious about a local girl named Joan and spent much of his time with her.

His flying was done primarily at Sky Harbor Airport in Northport, just west of Winnetka, and his goal was to accumulate hours so his aviation credentials would be impressive. Sky Harbor was a natural choice, as it was close to home and recently refurbished after a decline caused by the Great Depression that still lingered. When it was first built in 1929 the airport was considered a trendsetter, with an arched hangar for its service area and a deluxe terminal with a restaurant that was considered gourmet. Its public areas were luxurious and catered to the affluent flying public that was part of the well-to-do North Shore of Chicago. Frank worked on getting his private license at the same time. He remembered watching the 1933 air races from a nearby building, not having enough cash to get in the gate.

The Depression had not been kind to Sky Harbor; for several years it was virtually dormant, but as war loomed and the military took over part of its pilot training there, it sparkled once again and regained its position. It was at Sky Harbor that I took my first flight with the father of a Skokie School friend.

We saw some of Jim that year, 1940–41, but we learned about his departure for Canada only a week or so after he left. In those days the Army Air Corps required its pilot trainees to have a college degree, so it is my belief that Jim chose the Canadian route to get in the war and to do it in a plane.

This was in May of 1941, months before the U.S. faced its Pearl Harbor disaster and its entrance into World War II. The mood of the country was sympathetic to the British, but still very isolationist. Great Britain stood alone against the Axis powers of Germany and Italy, which had successfully invaded and conquered most of Europe. The Battle of Britain had begun in July 1940 and was officially ended on October 31. Dunkirk had fallen in June 1940, and France capitulated shortly after.

The Battle of Britain was the first modern European aerial battle, and its outcome was viewed as critical to the survival of the British Empire and a determinant of future war events. During the months of the fight, British Spitfires and Hurricane fighters took on the best the Luftwaffe could send. As the weary months drained both sides of their best planes and men, young men in America, particularly those in schools such as Riverside, with an aviation program, must have envied the glory and the fame these young fliers gained in their continual sorties against German bombers.

The Battle of Britain gave the British Isles hope for the future thanks to the bravery and skill of the young pilots in the Royal Air Force. Most of the stories and newspaper reports were incredibly admiring in their summary of the work done by the young pilots. The rest of the world too respected, if not admired, the pluck of the British, subjected to the daily bombings ordered by Herr Goering.

In a letter I received from my cousin Helen Cole she wrote, "Jim told his parents that he wanted to do his part in the war, but not kill anyone. The A.T.A. and C.N.A.C. gave him a chance to do that, and it was tragic that he lived such a short time in the effort."[3] Maybe Jim was thinking of his next move as he graduated, knowing something of the plight of the British and thinking of a way to help. Whatever that thought process was, I did not have a chance to share it with Jim as he gained more hours at Sky Harbor and partied with his many friends.

# 2

## Air Transport Auxiliary

In April 1941 Jim headed for Canada, determined to fly for the British. When he arrived in Montreal he met with officials of the Trans-Canada Air Lines who were acting as agents for British Overseas Airways Corporation (BOAC). Over several days of discussions he learned about the duties, the drawbacks, and the good things the British had to offer. BOAC was the agent for Air Transport Auxiliary (ATA), the ferry service that moved aircraft around the British Isles. Sometimes it was from the manufacturer to an airfield, sometimes from one airfield to another, and other times from the boat docks to airfields. Their jobs were to take newly manufactured planes and the planes provided by the American lend-lease program to scattered British fields, allowing Royal Air Force (RAF) pilots to pursue actual war duties.

By the time Jim would arrive in England, the Battle of Britain would be over but the German Luftwaffe would still be a threat to English cities and airfields, so flying military planes in the war zone would remain dangerous. But he loved to fly, and the chance to fly all these different airplanes, high-powered military airplanes, was a strong attraction. There was good pay, too: $50 per week plus $100 repatriation allowance, also once a week, both payable in U.S. dollars with no U.K. income taxes deducted. They would pay his passage to England from Winnetka and pay him $10 a day. There would be a $500 bonus at the end of the one year contract if all went well. And, finally, they would pay his passage home at the end of his contract, in addition to $100 travel expenses. It probably took him no time at all to accept the conditions; he signed his one-year contract in Montreal on May 22, 1941 as a second officer.[1]

Jim got his chance to fly different aircraft to different cities and airfields, in different weather conditions and dealing with different personnel. His records show the variety of aircraft: Moth, Harvard, Hurricane, Lysander, Spitfire, Swordfish, Blenheim Beaufighter, Beaufort, Fairchild, Wellington, and many others. Those included the tiny Moth, the bi-wing Swordfish, the powerful Spitfire, and the multi-engine Blenheim. For a twenty-year-old only one year out of high school it was a wonderful world.[2]

The ATA was formed virtually as the European war started in September 1939, while Jim was still marching across the parade grounds in Georgia. It was started by British Airways, which saw a need for this kind of service as the European clouds grew darker. It was never a military organization, but had its own uniforms, rankings, and procedures. The ATA welcomed women, in the early days with some reservations, but as time went on they became accepted as equal to men pilots. The ATA also welcomed Americans. In the war years 126 American men and 26 women would serve Britain in the ATA.

The ATA was the brainchild of Gerard d'Erlanger, a member of a well-known banking family and himself a director of British Airways. Even before the Nazi invasion of Poland he knew that nonmilitary pilots could be used to move aircraft from their manufacturing factories or their ports where lend-lease planes arrived, keeping the frontline RAF pilots on their primary job: fighting the war. At first only thirty pilots were selected, but over the coming months and years their ranks would grow to 1,152 men and 166 women, supported by flight engineers and radio officers. During the war 129 men and 20 women were killed. They would safely deliver 300,000 planes from their point of origin to the fighting bases where they could play their part in the war.[3] Eventually British Airways (later British Overseas Airways Corporation) found ATA's operations too much to handle in addition to its regularly scheduled flights, and throughout 1940–41 began to turn the organization over to the Ministry of Aircraft Production.

The ATA was first designed to fly the smaller aircraft, the Moths, to training facilities around the British Isles. And as it grew it welcomed women who were experienced pilots, although that program met with considerable resistance. Women were paid 20 percent less than men in the beginning, but in 1943 that was changed and all pilots were paid the same. Their duties were to pick up aircraft from manufacturing plants or repair centers and fly to a specified airfield. In the early days, in open cockpit planes, it could take up to a week to get an aircraft from English plants to Scottish airfields. There was to be no instrument flying; all flights were to be visual, with the ground always in sight. When the weather closed in, the delivery waited until the weather cleared—no exception. The weather in the British Isles is often nasty, and the instrument rule made for safer flying but erratic schedules. Many believed weather was the biggest danger for ATA fliers.

Another hazard present all over the British Isles was the barrage balloons, with their heavy steel cables, capable of tearing wings off unlucky planes. Many were near manufacturing plants, so they were a constant hazard to ATA pickup pilots. And for security reasons, balloon locations were not written on flight plans. The new or repaired planes seldom had any navigational equipment, and few had radios, so finding the right destination without communications and with nothing but a compass tested even the most experienced.

While RAF pilots trained for a specific aircraft, fighter, bomber, Spitfire, Hurricane, or Blenheim bomber, ATA pilots had to be able to fly any type of aircraft. Often manufacturers changed the location of certain cockpit instruments or controls, so even if a pilot had flown similar models recently, something might have changed on a newly assigned plane.

The most dramatic difference in controls was on the P-40. The model made for France required the throttle to be pulled out to increase power and pushed in to reduce power, just the opposite of other models. It would be like getting in a car that required the accelerator to be pushed down to slow and released to speed up. The pilots themselves invented methods to help when a new pilot entered his or her craft, such as displaying a card with the important variations in its performance, which would be prominently displayed.

A fact of life for these fliers was that they were virtual test pilots. They were the first to fly the newly manufactured airplane, and some planes being ferried from a repair facility to a field were not quite ready to return. Occasionally they were even recognized as dangerous, labeled NEA, "not entirely airworthy," on their way to be scrapped. To add to those dangers, in the early years of the war the RAF kept away many Germans planes, but not all, so there was a constant threat of attack both in the air and on the ground. This was the world that Jim entered shortly after his twentieth birthday, and a world he relished.

As the ATA grew, the original base at White Waltham Field (No. 1) became inadequate. Soon other pools began to be formed, some near manufacturing plants and others near airfields:

No. 2 Whitchurch, Bristol

No. 3 Hawarden, near Chester

No. 4 Prestwick, Scotland

No. 5 Luton, later Thame

No. 6 Ratcliffe, Leicester

No. 7 Sherburn-in-Elmet, Leeds

No. 8 Sydenham, Belfast

No. 9 Aston Down, near Stroud

No. 10 Lossiemouth, Scotland

No. 11 not named

No. 12 Cosford, near Wolverhampton

No. 13 not named

No. 14 Ringway, Manchester

No. 15 Hamble, Southampton

No. 16 Kirkbride, Solway Firth

All the pilots in pools at Hamble, Cosford, and Hatfield were women, but the other bases mixed the two sexes. Eventually there would be twenty-two pools in strategic locations. Jimmie began his training at No. 1 Waltham and was certified there for his ratings, but after that he spent his time headquartered at No. 6 Ratcliff, still flying all over the British Isles.

A factor that seemed important in the initial start-up was getting pilots back to their home pool, or base. They would take trains back, but in wartime, trains are inefficient and vastly uncomfortable. A pilot might take only two hours to deliver his or her craft but take two days to get home by train. So a taxi system was started, originally with a single-engine, two- or four-passenger plane, but often aircraft would go out in formation, so larger craft were needed to bring the pilots home quickly. The nine-passenger, twin-engine Avro Anson became the workhorse of the taxi program, sometimes carrying ten or twelve pilots back to base.

The ATC was a very British program, emphasizing a conservative approach to the ferry business. That's why a prank pulled by American pilot Gen Genovese in January 1942 almost caused his suspension. Transit aircraft were supposedly unarmed, but on this occasion Genovese and his friend Al Gingiss discovered that his Beaufighter guns were loaded, and the two began to look for targets on the coast of Scotland where they discovered several floating mines. They took turns spraying the target area, exploding mine after mine. Word eventually filtered back to officials at the British Ministry about these unidentified planes blasting the Scottish waters, and they were incensed. They posted an order that any such incident discovered in future would be grounds for immediate dismissal. The last sentence stated, "American pilots will pay particular attention to this order."[4]

It may have been this episode that caused Jim's discipline problems to begin. His ratings had been fine up until March 1942. He had been promoted to first officer Class C on September 18, 1941, meaning that he was qualified to fly single-engine aircraft, mostly fighters and high-performance planes. Then, on December 14, he was moved to Class B first officer, and after training given for Class 3 and 4 he was allowed to deliver light twin-engine planes. Finally, on that same day, he was given full authority to deliver all types of craft except four-engine and flying boats.

But he had been reprimanded back on October 24 and suspended for three days, losing £20, for a rather boyish episode involving "shooting up Ratcliff Hall," headquarters of his ATA Pool No. 6. Even so his commanding officer rated him "a keen and useful pilot." However, February 1942 proved his undoing. On the 17th he was blamed for taxiing on the frozen grass portion of a "runways-only aerodrome." The result of this indiscretion was that the Hurricane he was flying lost its tailwheel. Just eight days later he was held to blame for damaging a Spitfire when making an unauthorized flight: "pilot made careless approach & overshot." His record to date was enough for the ATA to demote him from first to second officer on March 6, and his evaluation by his CO on March 12 stated, "A hardworking and capable pilot but not always reliable. Now and again breaks from steady flying and indulges in low and dangerous flying and this has resulted in one accident."[5]

It took the ATA several days to decide that Jim was a risk they could not accept; his contract was terminated March 28, 1942, and he was sent back home. While in England he had flown 140.85 hours plus ten taxi hours in twenty-six different airplanes, and he was still just twenty-one years old. He sailed for home on the *Leticia* from Glasgow on April 8 with two other Americans, arriving in Halifax, Nova Scotia, on April 16. From there he headed for Winnetka and home. The crossing was not without considerable risk since German U-boats were causing huge shipping losses that year. Seventy-four Allied ships were sunk in the Atlantic by the German U-boats, which were still enjoying their "happy times!"

It is difficult to imagine how Jim managed to get his parents to agree to the ATA flying job. Great Britain was heavily involved in its war against Hitler, and the idea of their only son being a part of it must have worried them terribly. We seldom saw the Brownes in the months after Jim left, but we heard indirectly of the messages he sent from England, probably considerably tamed versions of events. I had started at New Trier the year he left and was mostly oblivious to the war in Europe, so my thoughts seldom turned to Jim in spite of the risks he was taking.

# 3

## China in the Past

Jim's next move brought him all the way to the other side of the world, to a place that was even more dangerous than Europe. As he waited for events to unfold in Winnetka, surrounded by his friends and family but itching to get back in the air, a visit from Pan American's Capt. Harold Sweet brought him new opportunities. They would come in China, a land of mystery and more than a little danger.

But as 1942 began, Jim was still in England, flying as much as he could and occasionally testing the patience of those in charge. At the time, most of us in the Midwest were more concerned with Hitler and his dramatic domination of Europe than we were with Japan's successes in China. The year would find Germany in the midst of a messy winter after its treacherous attack on Russia in June, and Britain would be standing alone as the rest of Europe fell to either the Nazis or Mussolini's fascists.

America in 1939–40 was not interested in participating in the wars of Europe, and even less in the war in Asia. Up until Germany landed troops in Poland in September 1939, many Americans had heard glowing reports of the remarkable recovery of Germany from the dark days following World War I.

I had some personal experience with that attitude from my grandfather Frederick Wilhelm Mehlhop, a second-generation German immigrant who still had family in the Fatherland. Bampa, my name for Granddad, had made a trip to Germany in the summer of 1937, following the death of my grandmother. Bampa was what I considered a typical German, somewhat aristocratic, erect and slim with a large gray mustache and a distinguished bald head. He lived with our family for seven years, so I got to know his moods and his habits and was constantly impressed with his rigid lifestyle. When dinner was not ready at six, his call could be predicted: "Katherine, dinner!" That used to drive Dad nuts, so Mom usually had dinner ready at the magic hour.

When Bampa came back from Germany in 1937, he announced that Hitler was the best thing that had ever happened to that country. "The trains are now running on time!" That was enough to satisfy Bampa that Germany was in good hands. It was many years later when he finally admitted that somehow Germany had run off the tracks. At that time, a large percentage of Americans were of German extraction, so there was much interest in the progress made there since Versailles, but questions began to emerge as the Germans began their expansion program. First Austria, then Sudetenland in Czechoslovakia, then the rest of Czechoslovakia in 1938. The British and French had conferred with Hitler and decided to have "peace in our time" by giving Hitler all of Czechoslovakia, in spite of the Czech government's protest. The Czech government was not even invited to the betrayal conference.

It was not until the invasion of Poland that America woke to the real goal of Germany: to sweep through all of Europe and, unknown to many at the time, sweep on into Russia in spite of the Nazi-Russian Non-Aggression Pact of August 1939.

But Jim's world would be in Asia, not Europe, as 1941 drew to a close.

In the ancient past, China and Japan had dealt mostly with their separate internal squabbles, between warlords in China and between militarists and conservatives in Japan, so if friction between the two countries existed, it was not much noted in the history books. But in the late 1800s, interest in Korea began to move Japan toward China's northern territories, with its vast open space and natural resources. And, much like today, in the late 1800s Korea sparked much of the unrest.

A few events in the late 1800s triggered unrest within Korea and increased China's concern that its influence in the affairs of that peninsula might suffer. In the 1880s China had dominated Korea and had been interested in its future. Japan had established a presence in Korea by then, sending a legation there to assist Japanese business ventures and citizens. In 1882 a food shortage and virtual Korean bankruptcy caused uprisings and attacks on the Japanese in the country. Tensions rose as both countries sent additional troops to support their positions, but a truce was finally called and the two sides relaxed.

In 1884 another dispute escalated but stopped just short of war. At the end of that so-called Gapsin Coup, another agreement was reached; this one called for the removal of all troops from Korea and a requirement that any reintroduction of military forces be announced before taking place. Both sides thought that would calm the nervous citizens and governments, but that was not to be.

In 1886 the Chinese fleet sailed to Nagasaki, Japan, for refitting and repairs. Chinese sailors menaced the town and rioting began. That escalated the anti-China feelings in Japan and laid the groundwork for more strain between the two nations.

Finally, in 1894 an actual war broke out over Korea in the Korean peninsula. It was called the First Sino-Japanese War and was fought primarily over Korea. The roots of that war were the events of previous years that increased tensions and the nationalist feelings of both Japanese and Chinese. At the time, Japan was well prepared militarily, having spent years sending its officers abroad to study, while the Chinese fleet was in disrepair and its troops were dispirited over poor pay and living conditions. The war lasted until 1895, and the Chinese lost their foothold in Korea, the island of Taiwan, and the Chinese city of Port Arthur. It was a humiliating defeat that marked the beginning of the end of the Sing Dynasty.

Japan's next confrontation was with Russia, when, in the War of 1904–5, the Japanese beat Russian forces and gave their newly formed military services even more confidence and arrogance. Their treatment of the lands they had subjugated—Korea and Taiwan—had been brutal and sadistic, earning them the hostility of those lands and peoples.

The only hiccup in the Nipponese expansion plan had happened several years before Pearl Harbor, on the borders of Russia, Manchuria, and Outer Mongolia. There a major struggle took place in a battle called Nomonhan, with Russia's Gen. Georgy Zhukov displaying the joint use of air, land, and armor as he fought the Japanese. The result was a significant defeat of the vaunted Japanese, whose basic weapon still consisted of dedicated infantrymen, not a good match against armor and air. It is interesting to note that the same tactics used by the Japanese against the Russians would be the tactics used in all their operations in World War II, tactics that doomed them to failure.[1]

The following years saw Japan's real push for Asian dominance, with its movement into Manchuria and subsequent war with mainland China. Japan was such a tiny land, yet its horizons grew beyond anyone's expectations.

We tend to think of World War II as beginning at Pearl Harbor in December 1941, but for China the war began with the invasion of Manchuria by the Japanese in September 1931. The Japanese claimed that the Chinese had blown up part of a Japanese-owned railroad in Manchuria, and they invaded to "protect Japanese economic interests" there. The issue is still in doubt as to who really blew up the railroad; some theorists believe it was young Japanese officers trying to provoke war. In any event Japan sent in troops and they were not resisted by the Chinese. From Manchuria, Japan's military program moved slowly into other Chinese territories.

China had been through centuries of warlords and dynasties, and a new attempt to unify its far-flung provinces seemed to defy a central government when Sun Yat-sen formed the Republic of China in 1912, which became known as the Kuomintang. After the death of Sun in 1925 the new republic struggled until 1928, when the Chinese National Party was formed. A new leader, Chiang Kai-shek, emerged to aggressively seek to centralize the government and unite the far-flung provinces of China as well as banish the increasingly aggressive Communist factions.

Chiang's biggest effort was a vigorous campaign to defeat local warlords who had established a semi-legitimate government in Beijing and were menacing the newly renewed Kuomintang. The campaign was a success, and the now powerful Kuomintang emerged as a significant organizer of a central government that included many of the wealthier provinces. The government center was in Nanking, where Chiang set up housekeeping. Chiang's bride, a member of the powerful Soong family, was a strong supporter of the generalissimo but also very independent. She developed a love for aviation, and in later years became the strongest ally of the American aviator and retired U.S. Army Air Corps captain Claire Chennault in a fractious era for control of Chinese air.[2]

Captain Chennault had long been an advocate of fighter tactics and had proposed new pursuit ship tactics, which unfortunately ran counter to the big bomber advocates in senior Air Corps ranks.[3] With his health issues, mainly hearing problems, his flying career in the army was coming to a close in the spring of 1937 when he met representatives from China at an air show in Miami. The Chinese were looking to build an air force as it coped with Japan's invasion, and so were recruiting Americans to lead the effort. It was Chennault's welcome chance to use his knowledge of tactics in actual combat situations.

According to Daniel Ford's book, Chennault resigned from the Air Corps on April 30, 1937 and went to China to begin a series of assignments that would result in his dream job, forming and leading a volunteer fighter command to be part of the Chinese Air Force but manned by volunteer American pilots. However, that was several years ahead; his first assignments were to teach young Chinese men the world of military aviation. In his early years in China he and Madame Chiang formed a bond that was instrumental in Chennault's success. Her support, sometimes without the generalissimo's consent, gave Chennault the power he needed.

Things became uneasy for Chiang as the Communist Party in China began to gain strength under Mao Zedong. The Kuomintang had originally included the Communist wing, but in the mid-1930s the Communists sought to structure their own party and left the KMT. Even after the loss of Manchuria, Chiang believed his principal enemy was the Communists rather than the Japanese who were steadily gaining villages in the north.

From 1931 to 1934 Chiang continued his campaigns to wipe out the Communists, and in 1934 had surrounded the Red settlement in Jiangxi in south-central China. The most dramatic move by the Communists was in 1934, when they began their Long March from south-central China north to Shaanxi Province, which included the now popular city of Xian. Red leader Mao and his second in command, Chou En-lai, in Jiangxi, determined to break out to join the Communist community in the North. On October 16, 1934, Mao led his Fourth Army of eighty-five thousand with fifteen thousand others through Kuomintang lines and they began their horrendous march. It took one year, covering six thousand miles, with pitched battles between the two forces all the way.[4]

The rest of the nation was angry as Japan increased their territory while the Chinese government troops were busy with the Reds. Finally, one of the former leaders in Manchuria, Zhang Xueliang, who had not been allowed to fight the Japanese in Manchuria, grew more and more frustrated with Chiang and decided to act. His troops surrounded the generalissimo's luxurious health resort in Xian, and on December 12, 1936, he arrested the Kuomintang leader.

The purpose of the arrest was to force the two Chinese factions to join together to combat the Japanese. Negotiations were finally concluded when Madame Chiang persuaded her husband to join the Reds in fighting Japan. It was an embarrassing time for the president of the Republic of China, but this move did unite the warring factions against China's main threat, Japan and called for the Reds' support of Chiang as both political and military leader of the united forces. But the relationship between Chiang and the Communists was fragile.

With negotiations ended successfully, the Boeing 247 carrying the generalissimo, his wife, and Zhang took off, piloted by an American named Royal Leonard. Later, Leonard became a CNAC pilot and a friend of Jim Browne.[5]

After the Xian incident, Zhang elected to return to Nanking with the Republic's leader, but when they arrived in Nanking, Chiang put him under house arrest, where he languished for more than fifty years. After the Communists took control of mainland China he was transferred to Taiwan, where he lived quietly until Chiang died in 1975. Zhang was finally released; he emigrated to Honolulu, where he became a Christian and died at age one hundred.

The Japanese had been steadily consolidating their Manchurian territory, gaining ground south of Manchuria and on islands off the China coast without much opposition as Chiang concentrated on the Communist Fourth Army. This allowed the Japanese to grow in arrogance and confidence and to create an incident that would begin a more open brand of warfare.

On July 7, 1937, Chinese soldiers lounged on the Marco Polo Bridge in Peking while Japanese soldiers patrolled nearby. It was reported that the Chinese had kidnapped one of the Nipponese soldiers, and tensions that had filled the city suddenly exploded. That was the beginning of the next phase of the Sino-Japanese conflict, and the Japanese were quick to move on military as well as diplomatic fronts.

Shanghai was a unique city, housing large numbers of foreigners in their own national settlements within the city. They were given broad rights by various treaties and agreements and lived for the most part peaceful, quiet lives. Japanese had the right to be there, as did British, French, Italian, and other nationalities, all protected by their own set of rules. The International Settlement was created by a series of treaties and was designed to keep foreign powers under control.

CNAC had their headquarters there, but after July 7, Japanese soldiers were aggressively moving through all settlements, upsetting everyone. In Peking a CNAC pilot bribed a farmer to hide him on his vegetable cart and take him to the airport, where he took his DC-2 to the air with no delay.

Air raids by Japan devastated Shanghai, made worse by Chinese Air Force bombers who mistakenly bombed the city. The war's effect on China was tragic, but the effect on CNAC was devastating as well. Two of its three routes were cut off, a number of planes had been confiscated by the Chinese Air Force, and their one remaining route to Hong Kong had lost its Shanghai anchor.

From then on it was chaos; Shanghai was evacuated, and Nanking was next. The Rape of Nanking still brings a sense of horror to those who read of the slaughter of the innocent. Wounded soldiers bayoneted, nurses and doctors beheaded, every woman spotted by the soldiers gang-raped—in short, every savage means of destroying a people was visited on the Chinese capital. It was evacuated, then Hankow was, and finally the Republic of China government headquarters moved to and stayed in Chungking. Throughout the moves inland newly released CNAC planes were evacuating as many of the locals as possible.

Chungking was a good city to be in when Japanese bombers rained down their explosives. The Yangtze River carved a large canyon and the banks on either side were lined with caves that provided protection from the bombers.

Kunming in southern Yunnan Province was becoming more important to CNAC and to the Chinese as the Japanese moved inland. However, it had no natural shelter for protection against Japanese bombers as it sat on the flat lands of Yunnan Province, surrounded by mountains and at an elevation of more than six thousand feet. Its citizens suffered terribly under continual bombardment from Japanese flying out of nearby bases.

Kunming was a French-influenced city, its streets lined with shady trees and strips of colorful flowers. It was hot and humid in the summer months, and its citizens suffered under the monsoon rains of those same months. By 1941 Kunming had become important as a transportation hub, allowing supplies to be brought in by the Burma Road, recently completed from Lashio, India. It also was the entry port for goods from India over routes discovered by CNAC in late 1941. Kunming's importance would only increase as Jimmie's role took shape.

# 4

## The Long Road to China

The events of Pearl Harbor and Germany's declaration of war against the U.S. had lit the fuse on American patriotism, and America was rising to the challenge of a two-front war. As 1942 began, Jim was still flying as much as he could, causing some concern among his superiors in England. The rather abrupt end to his flying days with ATA meant his return to Winnetka with almost celebrity status as a veteran of England's air war.

Events were moving in Jimmie's direction in July 1942, when Capt. Harold Sweet, a celebrated pilot of Pan American Airways and a veteran of many days with CNAC, visited Chicago on a recruiting trip. The details are sketchy, but he somehow connected with the Brownes and visited the Winnetka home as part of his recruiting duties. The Brownes seemed to like him, and he took to Jim as both a fine young man and a reasonably seasoned pilot for his age. I think he used the noncombat role of Pan Am as a vital part of the war effort, not like the band of killers so often pictured in aviation literature and films.

Actually, Sweet was recruiting for the Africa supply route under contract to Pan American Airways, and Pan Am was looking for pilots. It suited Jim's hopes to avoid combat yet play a part in the war, and even the family seemed to think that might keep him safe. After much conversation, about which I knew nothing, Jim agreed to go to New York for a physical exam and possible assignment to the Pan American Airways Africa run.

While he was in New York the Army Air Corps announced that it was canceling the PAA-Africa contract and would be making the Africa runs in army transports. Sweet had an alternative to offer, though: China National Aviation Corporation. The switch seemed to offer Jim an even more interesting opportunity; being part of the mysterious East appealed to him, so he agreed to sign on.

In New York he met several pilots, all of whom would play a part in his next few months. They were Charles Sharkey, Edward Leatherbury, and Alfred Oldenburg, all of them from the Royal Canadian Air Force; Richard Snell from the U.S. Navy; and Weldon Tutwiler from the Army Air Corps. Jim, from the ATA, made the sixth member. Snell and Jim passed their physicals with no problem, but Sharkey was sent back to Montreal to have dental work done.

Jim returned home to await the call from New York for hiring details; he was sent to Miami to find his transport to India, the western terminus for the infamous Hump route, China's only supply line. There had been a number of farewell parties before Jim left on September 23, 1942, none of which I was allowed to attend, being just sixteen at the time. But there a very tearful goodbye when Hadda and Brownie drove him to Chicago to board an Eastern Airlines flight to Miami. It was the last time they would see their son.

The six recruits met in Miami to wait for transport. Oldenburg kept a detailed log of their trip, neatly typed and with daily details. On the first page is an unsigned handwritten notation: "This was the first group hired thru Pan Am and just after Fly Tig [Flying Tigers] that went with CNAC."[1]

As the six boarded the C-53 in Miami for the first leg of their journey, a seven-hour flight to Puerto Rico, they were in high spirits. They might have sobered a bit if they knew that only three of them would live to come home. Jimmie, Tutwiler, and Sharkey all died in accidents in the coming months. But on September 27, 1942, they were off on a real adventure on their way to China.

The first day was devoted to getting acclimated to the crowded C-53, piloted by Captain Sweet, Jim's recruiter, with navigator

Dan Sheffield and James (Scotty) Scott. Along with the passengers and crew was enough cargo to make the cockpit accessible only by crawling on all fours. At one point their plane was challenged by two P-39s, but Sweet knew the proper password and the plane proceeded unmolested.

Arrival in Puerto Rico was on time, and hot showers were welcome. That taken care of, several went walking along the beach, then into town. There they learned that young ladies were available but venereal disease was epidemic, and they all seemed to shy away from trouble. Oldenburg's last note of the day was simply, "Browne bought a case of rum."

Next stop was Georgetown, British Guiana, about the same distance and duration as the day before. Oldenburg commented that cigarettes were 50 cents per carton, while Parker pen sets were $14.80. On the 29th they flew to Belém, Brazil, in six hours forty minutes. Sweet was letting the boys have some flight time so they could get a little experience in the type of plane they would be flying in China. That seemed to be a fine idea with the young flyers and was maybe a little sly on Sweet's part. In the afternoon they continued on to Natal, still in Brazil, where they stayed at a Pan Am Ferry House, which rated high with them, particularly the food. "Best since Miami and probably best on the trip," wrote Oldenburg. All had a good time.

On to Ascension Island, where there was little to enjoy. "Volcanic ash, no swimming because of sharks and strong undertow, water scarce and little entertainment," summarized their impressions. So no one was unhappy to take off for Accra on the African coast, where they were hosted by the RAF. That leg was more than ten hours, almost all over water, and proved to be pretty boring. They were hoping to see submarines, but no luck. In Accra they remarked on the nightshirt and fez that most men wore. Oldenburg wrote about the women there, "Saw African girls there. Up to age 15 they have nice figures but over 15 they get sort of droopy." These young men were very observant.

October 3 involved a flight from Accra to Kano, Nigeria. This was a war-time route that stayed over the water to avoid the Vichy French, the French forces that supported the Nazis after France surrendered. They controlled parts of the old French Africa and were considered a danger to Allied aircraft, thus the devious routing. The flight was low over African villages, which were a real novelty to the young Americans, and they wished they had a chance to see them from the ground. In downtown Kano, one of the oldest cities in Africa, was a copper mine and next to it an iron mine that sustained the town's semiprosperity. Kano also had a thriving market at the Nigerian Railroad station, and the crew bartered and haggled for items both useless and useful.

Here they got a glimpse of the power of medicine men, or voodoo priests. Oldenburg seemed startled when he wrote, "In the market, a voodoo man or native medicine man told a youngster he was going to die. The natives all got away from him and he fell to the ground. None of them would or could help him so he died." That was a shock to the young, naïve pilots.

Their stay in Kano was definitely one of the most interesting of the journey. They were held there for five hours, waiting so they could land in their next stop, Khartoum, Sudan, in daylight. They came to a bumpy stop on a soggy field in Khartoum, and had pancakes and syrup at an army camp. It was good, but not like Kano. They never did get to the town. The next day, October 5, they were off to Aden, Arabia, on a six-hour trip. They crossed over the Red Sea and the Arabian Desert, but apparently were unimpressed.

At Aden they were again guests of the RAF, but were leery of the food, and rightfully so. Their dishes left much to be desired, so after dinner, Oldenburg wrote, they brought out their emergency rations so they could survive. They slept late the next morning after testing the bar scene the night before, a disappointment, and then took the Pan Am Airlines car to city center. It turned out to be pretty interesting, because the city was known for its boatbuilding. Local history told of the construction of Noah's Ark here and the building of the Queen of Sheba's fleet. The city itself is built inside the walls of an extinct volcano, and the streets are designed for camels, not cars.

Masirah Island in the Arabian Sea was next, skirting present-day Yemen and arriving at the island just off the Oman coast to a dismal scene. The airport had been there for only a few months and there were but four RAF custodians, who shared their coffee and biscuits. On October 7 their trip was near an end as they took off for Karachi in present-day Pakistan, where prices were outrageous. They thought it was the presence of the U.S. and British armies that accounted for the high prices, so no one bought much of anything.

Last stop before getting to their destination, Dinjan, India, was in Calcutta, still on October 7. Oldenburg noted mostly its filth, its disease, and its utter disregard for human life. A streetcar was held up for quite a while when a leper fell on the tracks and was too weak to move. No one would go near him or help him, and eventually he crawled away. It was an eye-opening experience for the sheltered American youth.

According to Oldenburg's journal, they had covered twelve thousand miles in ten days; the passengers and crew were exposed to sights they probably never imagined: some impressive, some educational, and some exposing the more sordid sides of life outside the United States. From Calcutta it was on to Dinjan in northern Assam to learn about their new airline and the newly designed "lifeline of China," the notorious Hump.

# 5

## China National Aviation Corporation

As Jim in Winnetka looked toward his future, a new entity was about to enter his life. It was a little-known airline called China National Aviation Corporation. Today China National Aviation Corporation is known affectionately as CNAC, pronounced *Sea-knack*. Its history is unique to both China and aviation. Jim knew nothing about CNAC as he arrived home from England in April 1942, but the airline was looking desperately for American pilots to carry out its mission to aid China in the war against Japan. CNAC's history was a study of coping with wartime conditions, but the new conditions calling for Hump crossings on a massive scale were pushing the airline's limits.

The Republic of China had finally drawn some of the warlords of the Middle Kingdom together under one central government. Its leader was Sun Yat-sen, but his death in 1925 brought another name to the movement, Chiang Kai-shek. As the Republic was formed it included the Communist Party under Mao Zedong, but the marriage between the right-leaning Kuomintang and the far-left Communists did not last, and China began its long struggle between these two rival factions. Initially the Republic under Chiang was the stronger and became the face of China to the Western world.

One of the obstacles to governing far-flung districts was the lack of any modern transportation. Roads and railroad equipment were expensive, and building took years of preparation. One seemingly quick fix was air transportation; cheaper to establish and vastly faster, it seemed to be a way to bring the widely separated districts closer to the Republic's central government in Nanking. So the Republic of China granted charters to two airlines: Eurasia Aviation Corporation, which was aided by the German line Lufthansa, and China National Aviation Corporation, in partnership with America's Curtiss-Wright, a leading aircraft manufacturer.[1] It was 1929 and this partnership between the Chinese government and an American company was a pioneer in East-West relationships. Its survival was a surprise to many.

The structure called for the Chinese to have 55 percent ownership and Curtiss-Wright 45 percent; the Americans would be in charge of the operations, the Chinese in charge of finance and administration. The American management suffered in the first years until William Langhorne Bond was sent out in 1931 to save the investment. He was the right man for the job, as the future proved; he was not a seasoned pilot but a brilliant manager.

The China of those early days was in every sense a slumbering giant. Its industrial power was just being harnessed, but its feudal system and wide disparity of wealth was a holdover from the days of emperors and dynasties. Certain families controlled much of the wealth, and certainly much of the power. One such family was the Soongs, many of whom would play leading roles in the Chinese fight against Japan and in support of aviation in its early days.

Chiang was eager to have a successful airline as he chartered the two new lines. He separated their authorized routes, with Eurasia given the rights to the middle of the country while CNAC was afforded three routes primarily along the seaboard. The first and primary path was Shanghai to Hankow along the Yangtze River. This was reasonably easy to establish since the Yangtze and other swamps and bodies of water would replace the immediate need for airfields. The route would soon be extended on to Chungking, then to Chengdu.

CNAC's first manager, Harry Smith, was not the right man in many ways, but he selected probably the best airplane for the fledgling airline, the Loening Air Yacht. It was cumbersome-looking, with two-wings and a cabin behind the wings with the single radial engine mounted between wings directly above the two-man open cockpit that sat in front of and above the passenger cabin. It seated six courageous passengers and was an amphibian, capable of landing virtually anywhere. Later they took off the wheels and made use of the Yangtze's flooded banks, landing on the adjacent swamps and bogs.

Not only did Smith find the right plane, but he found the right number two man, Ernest Allison. Allison joined CNAC in September 1929 with a varied aerial background that started with Army Air Corps training, then work as an air mail pilot and a barnstormer, bringing eight thousand hours of flight time to the virginal aviation enterprise of CNAC. Early in his army career he had saved Claire Chennault from washing out of the air corps flight school, and he would maintain a lifelong friendship with the general.[2] Allison became CNAC's highly qualified senior pilot.

Smith had made several good decisions, but he never accepted the Chinese as real partners. When Bond was appointed to succeed him, Bond brought a new respect for the role of the Chinese, which he then demanded from all his flight personnel. That was much of the secret of CNAC's success. Although there were bitter confrontations between senior Chinese and Bond, these always seemed to be resolved before they caused major damage.

The U.S. was having its own troubles in the late 1920s and 1930s; the Great Depression caused many businesses to close as profits shrank to impossible lows. Curtiss-Wright was not exempt from the struggle during those dark days, and their fledgling airline in China was of no help. Curtiss-Wright was a manufacturer of airplanes and had no experience running an airline. In 1933 it was seeking a buyer for the line, and the visionary Pan Am president Juan Trippe was looking to extend his Pacific presence and saw CNAC as a great opportunity. So in 1933 Pan Am tied itself to China's destiny.

CNAC management opened the required second route, Shanghai to Hankow to Peiping in the north, in late 1933. At the same time, a new face appeared in the picture, Harold Bixby from New York, representing Pan Am's interests. Bixby and Bond formed a warm personal and professional relationship that lasted throughout the turbulent years of CNAC's existence. There were a few hurdles in the northern run, but Allison used six high-wing Stinson planes that would carry four passengers plus the pilot and copilot. The line became operational but was hardly profitable, in fact chewing into the profits made on the lucrative Yangtze run.

New faces were adding to Allison and Bond's meager flight crews: Stan Kaufman; Birger Johnson; Eric Just, the German fighter pilot; Cecil "Pop" Sellers, a World War I bomber pilot; Robert Gast; and Paul Baer. Some stayed on for years, others drifted away, and others met their fate during their China stay.

As the deadline for authorizing Route Three, Shanghai to Canton, approached it was decided to go for it. It would be different than the other two routes—it would be a Pan Am operation, not CNAC's, and it would have new two-engine S-38 Sikorsky planes to fly the dangerous cliff-lined coastal path. The first flight carrying passengers ended in disaster, wiping out one of the three S-38s, but at least no one was killed. A second attempt was made on April 10, 1934, in marginal weather that turned bad almost immediately, and the S-38 crashed into the fog-shrouded bay. Only Bob Gast's body was found of the four on board. So Route Three was shut down.

But it reappeared soon after with a significant change. It would be a CNAC operation, not a Pan Am route. The early days of Route Three were full of tragedy. The loss of Gast and his crew was coupled with the earlier S-38 crash. Then, on January 19, 1934, Mrs. William Grooch, the wife of the original pilot of Route Three, climbed to the eighth floor of their apartment building and, holding her two sons in her arms, leaped to their deaths.[3] Grooch was almost mad with grief and shortly after was transferred back to Pan Am in Florida.

To add to that carnage, an S-38 the previous year had stopped at the Shanghai airport just for the night. Flown by Christy Mathewson, son of the famous New York Giants pitcher, and accompanied by his wife, they left their plane with CNAC personnel for the night. The next morning on takeoff something terrible happened to the controls and the plane rose briefly, then plunged into the murky Huangpu River. Both the Mathewsons were killed. The gods seemed to have unleashed their fury on the enterprise.

China was in a difficult period on September 19, 1931, when the Japanese responded to an incident in Manchuria, where Chinese had allegedly bombed a Japanese-owned train. Japanese troops then spread across Manchuria and shortly afterward set up the puppet government of Manchukuo. The Chinese organized boycotts of Japanese goods, which were effective, but in the meantime Japanese from warships in the Shanghai area fought the Chinese 19th Army until March 1932, when the fighting sputtered to a close, leaving the Japanese peering into northern China from their perch in Manchukuo. Having won Shanghai, they were preparing to move up the Yangtze to take the river cities. The Chinese Army fought bravely in those first months of open warfare but were no match for the well-trained Japanese troops.

The Shanghai fighting briefly interrupted the Shanghai CNAC operation, but the Manchurian incident did not interfere with the operations in the North, leaving Routes One and Two busy and now profitable. Mixed in with the Japanese insertion in the China scene was the continuing fighting between Chiang's Kuomintang forces and the Communists under Mao, still contesting the Republic's right to rule. Route Three had overcome its infancy and was now operating, first to Canton, then to Macau, and finally to the real attraction, Hong Kong. There were even some profits by 1935.

In that year the Chinese government requested a new line be opened between Chungking and Kunming to draw in the southern provinces. There was little knowledge at that time of the importance of the new terminal in Kunming. The new line featured newly acquired Ford Tri-motors, which experienced their own set of problems on the early runs, but the line was a success within a short period and CNAC showed signs of prosperity, pleasing Pan Am, Bixby, and Bond.

April 28,1937, was probably one of aviation's most historic days: the first Philippine Clipper arrived in Hong Kong, completing its flight from San Francisco via Honolulu, Midway, Wake, Guam, and Manila. The first flight was made by the regal, four motor S-42, a

Sikorsky-made thing of beauty.[4] The Clipper then went on to complete its flight to Shanghai, where celebrations were long and loud.

It was only days later when the Asian world exploded. On July 7, 1937, Japanese troops in Peiping and in Shanghai began the invasion to the interior of China. It was called the Marco Polo Incident since it started on the Marco Polo Bridge in Peiping, but the Japanese imperial forces were primed for the invasion, with their air force leading the way. The effects on CNAC were immediate and dramatic. CNAC pilot Foxie Kent was in Peking getting ready to return to Chungking when he found out the Japanese were all over the city.

Kent's abrupt departure ended the Shanghai-Hankow-Peiping Route, and in August an evacuation of Shanghai began as the city was overrun by the invaders. Shanghai was a disaster, mistakenly bombed by Chinese Air Force bombers trying to hit a Japanese cruiser on the Huangpu River, turning the city into a slaughterhouse. For CNAC, it was a disaster. The Chinese Air Force impounded most of CNAC's planes, and tensions ran high everywhere.

Nanking fell on December 13, 1937, and the resulting Japanese entry into the treasured old city was a bloodbath in which the dead outnumbered even those killed in atomic blasts of later years. There was no official count, a task too grisly for anyone to undertake, but the term "Rape of Nanking" covered more atrocities than the human mind can absorb. CNAC made few flights out of the ravaged city; Royal Leonard made the last. As Leonard left on his final flight out of Nanking he told his copilot Wong it almost looked as if the world were on fire. Wong's grim reply was "Plenty of fire. Nanking is torch. Torch may one day set world on fire."[5]

During these grim days, Bond was in New York meeting with Trippe and senior Pan Am officials. Trippe declared that CNAC was dead and Pan Am wanted out of China's bedlam. Bond argued that it was the time to stay. Finally, Trippe relented and Bond caught the next Clipper back to China. But Bond put his whole future into his agreement to stay. He would resign from Pan Am and keep his role at CNAC, as would all Pan Am staffers currently in China. The Chinese Air Force had taken almost all CNAC planes except for one DC-2 then in Hong Kong. Without planes and without revenue Bond had to let his loyal fliers go. Hal Sweet and Harry Smith, who had been fired years before but was recently rehired, elected to stay with CNAC, and two other old-timers, Chuck Sharp and Hugh Woods, elected to "vacation" in Indonesia and wait for developments. So it looked very much as if Bond had won his battle with Trippe but was losing his war. When Bond returned to China, he ordered all flights canceled and terminated all pilot contracts.

In an almost impossible gamble, using every contact he had made in his six years with the airline, Bond was able to get his aircraft back from the Chinese Air Force and once again create an effective airline to aid China in its losing cause. The Chinese armies had been no match for the Japanese military machine, and Japanese moved south from the Manchurian border and west from Shanghai. The ring around China was gradually closing, shutting it off from the outside world and the vast quantities of supplies it needed to survive. To show the Chinese that Bond was in complete control, Bixby remained in the Philippines, acting only as an observer on the China scene. Fortunately, Woods and Sharp came home to CNAC's new headquarters at Hong Kong and immediately began flying the routes that were reopening.

At the time, though, few thought CNAC would survive; Chairman Trippe was pushing hard to get out of China, and Bond was the lone voice maintaining that this was the time to stay. The airline was needed desperately as evacuation of coastal cities would be necessary, and CNAC would be at the forefront. Trippe finally gave in to Bond's persistence and agreed to hold off for a bit, but Bond had to show some great results, soon, if he were going to be allowed to stay.

Bond then performed his magic. He brought the pilots he had terminated back to Kunming and was able to talk the Chinese into returning the CNAC planes. New headquarters were established at British-controlled Hong Kong. But the price was high: the Chinese military was now running the airline.

It was only a month or so after the Chinese Air Force took over airline controls that it occurred to them they had no idea how to run an airline. Things were going haywire in the operational end of the business. So, the man in charge, Col. Lem Wei-shing, basically left the scene and stayed away. Bond was back in control.

Japanese ground forces were moving westward, and Hankow lay directly in their path. It was apparent that the city would fall. CNAC was informed that it would be evacuated on October 25, 1938, and CNAC would be needed. And needed they were, with the thousands of citizens and military all seeking a way to stay in front of the Japanese. Stories of the Rape of Nanking had filtered to Hankow, and there was no doubt what their treatment would be if they were captured.

CNAC staff had prepared for the onslaught and kept strict crowd control. The older Consolidated Commodores were relegated to the short hops, stopping at Yichang to refuel, and two of the new CNAC captains, Hugh Chen and Moon Chin, piloted the aircraft into Hankow. The DC-2 pilots were carrying full loads, and pilots were wearing out. Leonard flew for thirty-six hours straight, then was ordered to bed. Sharp was alternating with him and was able to snatch a few hours of sleep between roundtrips. The last to depart were the most important: Chiang Kai-shek and Madame Chiang.

China was being encircled by Japanese-held territory, Manchuria, the islands of the west coast, and coastal ports, with the exception of Hong Kong. With the Japanese takeover of Indo-China a Hanoi rail connection was cut off. In 1937 it was decided to build the Burma Road, which, it was hoped, would allow for some supplies to be delivered by road. It started in Burma at Lashio, wound snake-like over the hills and mountains of the Himalayas and was to terminate in Kunming. Its construction was an engineering miracle; when it was completed in 1938 it had three hundred bridges and three thousand culverts on its 726-mile length, all built by hand.

After opening the Burma Road in 1938, the British bowed to Japanese pressure and closed it in 1940, but it was reopened a year later. At its best it could do little to maintain the necessary flow of goods to needy China, meaning that at that time CNAC was China's only hope.

Fortunately some of the pilots who had left when the war broke out returned to fly the planes recovered from the Chinese Air Force.

Moon Fun Chin was one example. Born in China, he and his father, who had gained U.S. citizenship by a rather ingenious method, emigrated to China and Moon Chin was hired as a mechanic by CNAC, "the Middle Kingdom Space Family," as the Chinese called it. That was in 1935, and Moon Chin, later a full-fledged captain, remained part of the airline family until 1946, when he branched out to cofound the Central Air Transport Corporation.

Moon Chin was still with Bond's virtually new airline, as were Woods and Sharp. Allison had left, Eric Just also, and several others as well. Leonard was back, waiting for trouble ahead. To add to the returnees, Chennault had to close his flying school, which had been in Hankow, and moved to Chungking. He lost some of his pilots to CNAC as the flight school reduced its mission. That is when Bill McDonald joined, leaving Chennault's school, then Emil Scott, Walter "Foxie" Kent, Frank Higgs, Bob Pottschmidt, and Syd DeKantzow from Australia. There was one name, Zigmund Soldinski, that appeared when Pan Am sent its crews to aid in establishing the infamous Route Three. He had remained ever since, leaving Pan Am employment to stay with the chancy CNAC. Sol was a lead mechanic, a true genius with aircraft, and largely responsible for keeping battered planes aloft.

September 1939 shattered the world with Germany's attack on Poland and the lowlands. That event ended the possibility of peace that had been a distant hope, as negotiations among Germany, France, and Great Britain had been feeding that fading dream. The immediate effect in China was the termination of Eurasia, the German line that had been formed in 1929 with CNAC. Other than that there was little change in everyday life.

Bond had a fairly severe heart attack, which had much more impact on CNAC than the invasion of Poland, in September 1939. His condition was critical to the CNAC world. Bixby issued an order to Bond to get to New York immediately, for business reasons ostensibly, but really to seek medical help. Bond was not at all reluctant and left immediately for the U.S.

Bond had left Sharp in charge of CNAC operations, and things were moving well. The stalwart Woods was gone, resigning after another close call, but the new DC-3 had arrived, giving everyone a boost. It could transport twenty-one passengers in comfort. Life was assuming a welcome normalcy. Of course it couldn't last.

Chennault had been in China for several years, heading the China Air Force and overseeing several American-led flight schools. As the various territories in which he operated were lost to the invaders, his training schools had moved. But he had a dream that he could recruit, train, and take into battle a group of experienced American pilots who could augment the rather woeful Chinese Air Force.

He festered, having nothing to do after he left Hankow, so he went to the U.S. to lobby for his self-named American Volunteer Group, although history would record them by their popular name, the Flying Tigers. CNAC and the AVG would be critical to each other, CNAC flying in the gas, ammunition, and spare parts while the AVG tore into unsuspecting Japanese planes.

Chungking was a rather desperate city in which to locate the Republic of China's bureaucracy. It was entirely rural, had no industry, and was hundreds of miles from the nearest railroad. In addition to its own problems, it now housed hundreds of thousands of refugees from Yangtze River cities and villages, scared to death of falling into Japanese hands. For CNAC, Chungking's air facilities were hardly adequate. The main landing area was an island in the Yangtze that would disappear under sixty feet of water during monsoon season. Add to that the regular air attacks that forced many to live in caves along the river. With all the addition of government and refugees, it wasn't hard to imagine what conditions were for the people of Chungking. But this is where the Chinese retreat ended. The Japanese knew that taking Chungking would be costly and accomplish little strategically. But they still bombed it on a regular basis.

It was here, though, that Bond met the most fascinating person on the scene: Madame Chiang Kai-shek. He had been hoping to meet her and had made that suggestion to several officials, but nothing ever developed. Suddenly W. H. Donald, an Australian in the generalissimo's employ, called on him and said that Madame would be available to meet him the next day. When Bond was introduced, he was struck by her beauty—her hair, her eyes captivated him, and he was even more flattered when the generalissimo himself gave him a few minutes. He told Bond that if he encountered any problem at all to let him know. That was very impressive.

One of CNAC's shining moments came on May 20, 1941, when Woods was piloting the DC-3 from Hong Kong to Chungking. He landed without incident, then took off for Chengdu with twenty-two passengers. He received a warning that Japanese planes were near Chengdu, so he changed course to Suifu, landing there, and hustled his passengers to safety. Sure enough, bombers appeared overhead and soon bombs were falling all around them. Only one hit the DC-3, but it went straight through the right wing, virtually tearing it off the fuselage. The damaged DC-3 would need a complete new wing if it were to fly again. This daunting problem was dumped onto the lap of Sol Soldinski in Hong Kong, who decided to share the problem with Managing Director P. Y. Wong.

The problem was that the only wing available was from a DC-2, and there was much discussion about the possibilities of attaching the smaller DC-2 wing to the DC-3 aircraft. The problem seemed to be solvable, they both agreed after draining part of a bottle of White Horse Scotch. After several experiments, it was decided that the wing could safely be attached, but the next problem was how to get it from Hong Kong to Suifu.

The solution was to find a qualified pilot who would share the White Horse and agree to the flight. So, Sol slung the smaller wing under another waiting DC-2 and put the proposition to Hal Sweet. A little White Horse, and Sweet was ready to go. Then they discovered that sales had sold all seats on the flight to Chungking in the DC-2, which would overload by 2,200 pounds. Nevertheless Sweet fearlessly said, "I'll fly it!" And he did. He took the rescue DC-2 with the DC-2 wing slung below, full of passengers, to Chungking, then went on to deliver the wing to the damaged DC-3 in Suifu. Repairs were made, and Sweet flew the repaired aircraft to Hong Kong, after picking up a full load of passengers in Chungking. And so was born the DC-2½.

The airfield in Kunming was now assuming more importance, and it would become even more so as the years progressed. It was located over a mile high, six thousand feet, and had as a climate rather warm, humid air. Not the greatest combination for the overloaded, overworked transports of the day. It was not only the airport conditions that caused problems; there were Japanese fighter bases in Indochina that were too close for comfort. The French had given up in Asia, and the Japanese were quick to take advantage of the possibilities. They began installing military equipment in the areas where they felt it would be useful, beginning in French Indochina, now known as Vietnam.

In one of CNAC's most significant contributions, Bond and his pilots in November 1941 created and plotted several routes over the mountains from Dinjan, in India's northeast section, to Kunming, routes that became the highways in the sky that would bring the fully loaded airplanes needed to feed the giant Chinese needs. The U.S. Air Corps was convinced the job could not be done by air, yet there was no alternative as the Japanese continued to shut down land routes.

The big blow was just ahead and coming fast. All through the Far East was the certainty of war, yet how and who the Japanese would attack was unknown. Even as far back as 1919, when American troops were sent to the Russian Far East and mingled with the arrogant and brutal Japanese troops who commanded them, there had been a certainty that the U.S. and Japan would clash. In later years, with constant border incidents along the Russian-Chinese border, the Japanese military considered moving on Russia, which was undergoing one of Stalin's periodic purges. Some leaders in Tokyo spoke of the Go North policy, attacking Russia's Siberia and gaining vast natural resources, plenty of expansion room, and access to Europe.

But a little-known battle called Nomonhan in Outer Mongolia in 1939 popped that balloon when the Japanese were soundly defeated by the Russians under General Zhukov. From then on, all efforts were directed toward planning drives on the American Fleet and the resources of the Southeast Asian countries.[6]

The result of all that planning became evident on December 8, 1941, in the East, December 7 in the U.S. The whole-scale bombings took place on Southeast Asian cities—Hong Kong, Malaysia, Singapore, Manila, and the Hawaiian island of Oahu. The results were particularly devastating for CNAC when the bombers hit Hong Kong.

Pan Am's Capt. Fred Ralph was in Hong Kong, having brought his Pan Am Hong Kong Clipper to the Kowloon Pan Am dock. He was wakened by calls that were confusing and contradictory. Finally, Bond got him on the phone and, knowing we were now at war, told him to fly immediately to Kunming and land on the lake there. Virtually at the same time the air raid sirens went off and bombs began falling. Ralph managed to get to safety with CNAC personnel just in time to see planes with the Japanese Big Red Ball open up on the Clipper. The first passes only put a few holes in her, but eventually the gas tanks were hit, and the flames quickly engulfed the whole aircraft.

At Kai Tak airport in Kowloon, bombers and fighters were tearing up anything on the ground, mostly airplanes. CNAC planes were taking a terrible beating. Capt. Emil Scott was there, worried about his wife in Manila, and he was joined by Woods, who had recently rejoined the airline, and Sharp. Leonard had just left for the States on his annual leave, but other pilots—Cecil Sellers, Pop Kessler, and Frank Higgs—were there. A tally of all planes lost included two DC-2s, two Condors, two Junkers, two RAF seaplanes, one Wildebeest, and the Hong Kong Clipper. The good news was that in the hangar and undamaged were two DC-3s, one DC-2, one Condor, and one Eurasia Junker. And one DC-3 inbound to Hong Kong coming from Rangoon with Bill McDonald.[7]

Bond had been caught on Hong Kong Island, while most of the others were at Kai Tak, watching the debacle. Sharp and Woods were at the airport, and it fell to them to organize the confusion and bring about an evacuation of CNAC staff and as many others as could be handled.

With bombers still overhead and wreckage all about them at the airport, it was decided to shuttle passengers to Namyung first, then, when everyone had been taken out of Hong Kong, the shuttles would take them on to Chungking. To do this there were five planes, two DC-3s, one DC-2, one Condor, and a Eurasia Junker. But there was also McDonald's DC-3 arriving from Rangoon later that night.

Bond was back in Hong Kong with the almost impossible chore of selecting passengers for each plane. These included Mrs. Kung, wife of the finance minister and sister to Madame Chiang, and some other high-placed locals. Bond was able to use his diplomatic skills, and boarding began late on the 8th.

The last plane left with Bond on December 10, a DC-2 flown by the ever-present Moon Chin. On December 15 Chungking newspapers claimed 275 people had been evacuated in one of the most perilous bits of work in the history of aviation. The operation had taken its toll on Bond, who had been burned by acids in the wreckage of the hangar, and with his heart condition had everyone concerned. Still, with all the confusion and occasional bitterness, CNAC had performed admirably and was again on the right side of public sentiment.

Jimmie was still in England when the Japanese hit Pearl Harbor. While there is no record of his thoughts that day, he must have been somewhat satisfied that he had seen it coming and had had the courage to do something about it. From all reports, Britain was sympathetic to the disaster but overwhelmingly grateful that America would now be in the fight.

The war brought new lend-lease C-47s and DC-3s to Dinjan, and former airline pilots and ground crews came to CNAC from the AVG and the United States. CNAC became a vital part of the transportation network feeding the planes, the mills, and the people of China. During those war days there was a large increase in staff at CNAC. The original pilots had had thousands of hours of flight time, but as the lend-lease planes arrived, crews had to be found using pilots who did not have such extensive flight records.

Interestingly, the largest group of pilots ever recruited by CNAC was the group from the AVG. There had been much bitterness over the treatment of the veteran combat pilots by the Air Corps, primarily because of the attitude of Brig. Gen. Clayton Bissell. His unyielding refusal to grant regular commissions to the pilots was a deterrent, and CNAC's offer to all was tempting. CNAC records in the Pan Am Collection at the University of Miami show that nineteen of the veterans went to work for CNAC, while only five elected to return to the Air Corps.

The Air Corps finally accepted that use of the newly established air routes was necessary, and as CNAC was using the routes they had established, the Air Corps, using those CNAC routes, began Hump crossings in April 1942. In its first few months of Hump crossings, CNAC carried 4,700 pounds of cargo, compared to 3,500 pounds of cargo by the Air Corps. In July the newly formed Air Corps Air Transport Command hauled 73 tons with thirty-five planes and CNAC brought in 136 tons using nine planes.[8]

That was hardly enough to supply the Chinese, fighting a massive Japanese Army, but it was a beginning. Much later, in August 1944, according to Greg Crouch's book *China's Wings*, ATC delivered 23,675 tons of material to China, and 22,314 in September, and CNAC added 1,000 tons more. At war's end, CNAC was bringing about 10 percent of the ATC's tonnage, with vastly fewer planes, pilots, and airfields.[9]

But it was the men who made it all work; many of them became legends in the aviation world. The pilots were a mixed breed; some characters were of the classical kind, some were quiet and cautious, some were gregarious and fun-loving, but courage was the common denominator. To fly the Hump in 1942–43 took plenty of that, knowing the many ways the hills could kill you.

This was the life that the six new pilots had signed up for, and after their weary journey and the sights of the primitive quarters and facilities in Dinjan in these days of 1942, they may have had a few reservations. But all six stayed until relieved, and three stayed forever.

# PART 2

## THE FATAL FLIGHT

# 6

## The Flight

Not much specific information remains today on Jimmie's flight of November 17, 1942, from Dinjan, CNAC No. 60's home field, to Kunming, the Chinese Hump base. Dinjan was newly constructed in Upper Assam in northern India, over the tea plantations of the area. The runways were laid with much primitive Indian and Chinese labor, using crushed rock for the base, then repeatedly rolled over by huge stone-rollers pulled by the natives, harnessed sometimes in the hundreds. The finished product was surprisingly good and provided solid footing for not only the cargo planes but B-25 and B-24s that were periodically stationed there.

It is worthy of note that the flying CNAC was doing was probably the most dangerous sort, including combat tours, anywhere. Every flight was a potential disaster; there were no "milk runs" over the Himalayas. And CNAC No. 60's two pilots were not seasoned transport pilots. John Dean had been trained on single-engine fighters, dive-bombers, and torpedo planes in the U.S. Navy, while Jim had had some time in multi-engine bombers when he flew for the ATA, but his total time in twin-engines was probably less than one hundred hours. Dean had been flying for CNAC for several months, but his flight time in C-47s was probably also low.

On November 17, 1942, CNAC No. 60 was loaded in Dinjan with aviation gas and medical supplies needed by the fighter squadrons at Kunming. The plane was probably overloaded by some 3,500 to

4,000 pounds, which was normal for all Dinjan-Kunming flights. The summer monsoons had passed, and the airstrip was dry and hard, but the weather was still hot and humid. No record can be found of exact takeoff time, but it likely was shortly after sunup, the best time to have the sun burn off the early haze.

Dean was in the left seat, Jim in the right, and K. L. Yang sat behind Dean on the radio set up against the wall of the cockpit. Other planes were getting ready to leave, too, as No. 60 received clearance for takeoff and sped down the runway out over the Brahmaputra River, taking either the northern route up toward Fort Hertz, Burma, or the southern route toward Yunnan Yi. The flight was about 550 miles and took almost four hours on a normal day, and all signs pointed toward this one as normal. As they landed in Kunming, Chinese workers immediately began unloading the aircraft and getting ready to load tin ingots for the trip back to Dinjan.

While the Hump was known for its lifesaving supplies of gasoline, spare parts, medical needs, and other war-time requirements, it is not well known that the return flights also carried loads, but on these return trips the cargo was mostly tin, tungsten, silk, and even hog bristles. The sale of these goods raised important funds for the Chinese to buy what they needed.

According to Gen Genovese in his book, *We Flew without Guns*, another C-47 from Dinjan had landed that morning with pilot Robert Raines and copilot Genovese. Their plane was being unloaded as well, so the crews headed for the operations shack, where chief pilot Bob Pottschmidt was keeping track of flights. Pottschmidt's group in the operations shack in Kunming was an interesting mix: there was Pottschmidt, a CNAC veteran of five years in China; Raine's crew; and Dean's. Raine and Dean were both about to finish their first year in China and their fourth month with CNAC. They were from the AVG, the Flying Tigers, who had fought the superior Japanese air forces from December 1941 until the AVG was disbanded on July 4, 1942. Both had three Japanese air victories in the hectic air battles over Burma and China, Dean with the 1st Squadron, the Adam and Eves, Raine with the 3rd Squadron, the Hell's Angels. They had elected to stay in China with CNAC rather than return to the U.S. with offers from General Bissell. The copilots, too, had similar backgrounds. Both had flown in England for the Air Transport Auxiliary, ferrying all makes of aircraft from factories to airfields throughout the British Isles. For various reasons their contracts had ended in the spring of 1942, and they had been sought out by CNAC's parent company, Pan American Airways.

All four had one common bond: they had all been fighting on two widely separated fronts even before Pearl Harbor. And they were young: Genovese, Raine's copilot, was twenty-five; Raine himself was twenty-four; Dean was twenty-six; and Jimmie, Dean's copilot, was just twenty-one.

The third member of a CNAC crew was in most cases a Chinese radio operator. When CNAC was first chartered in 1929 it was decreed that all pilots and copilots would be American, or Caucasian, but the radios would be operated by Chinese radiomen. So, Dean's crew included Kuan Liu Young, carried on the roster as K. L. Yang.

Jimmie and Genovese had experienced the hazards of British air in their days with ATA in 1941. Jim had left England in March 1942, and Genovese in June. When Genovese signed up for CNAC he and several others were in New York and were contacted by a young lady who asked if they would be seeing Jim. She had read in the paper of new pilots going to join CNAC in China. Genovese was happy to assure her that he and Jim would be together soon. She had a package delivered to Genovese and explained that it was a stuffed animal, an elephant, meant to bring good luck to Jim in the hazardous flying ahead. Her name was Joan, she was from Chicago, and she and Jim had become engaged just before he left in September. So the elephant, later named Tarfu, began his long journey with Genovese.

As the two crews and their chief pilot waited for the loading to be completed, Raines and Dean reminisced about their aerial fights with the Japanese. Listening to two of the real combat veterans relive their victories and near misses was a chance not to be missed. Genovese was happy to see that Jim had brought Tarfu, who lay snuggled up to him.

Conversation stopped suddenly when Pottschmidt's phone jingled with a call from the air raid signal tower: "Okay, boys, get 'em off the ground. Three bombers heading this way!" Standing CNAC orders were for planes to get airborne whenever the enemy approached, so the two crews rushed out the door. Raine's plane was still having a few repairs made, but Dean's had just finished loading and was ready to leave. His plane was overloaded with roughly 27,000 pounds of tin ingots and some hog bristles. For some reason the Chinese hog bristles were especially suited for several types of war uses. As they dashed out, Dean said he thought they would head right for Dinjan instead of coming back to Kunming. Potty reported that there was lots of ice up north, but there were Japanese fighters from Burma bases on the southern route. According to Genovese, Dean elected to go the northern route.

CNAC No. 60 spun around to the end of the single gravel runway and began its takeoff roll at 9:05 GMT (5:05 p.m. local time); weather reported as foggy and deteriorating, with temperatures in the mid-50s and winds a negligible 6 miles per hour. The Kunming airport was at more than six thousand feet, so foggy, dense air at that altitude made the takeoff run a long one for the overloaded C-47. Eventually the plane lifted off, the gear went up, and it disappeared forever into southern skies.

As Raine and Genovese came back to the shack, the first thing Gen saw was Tarfu. "Standing there looking very forlorn, with his big ears sticking out and his trunk hanging down almost to the cushions, was the little blue elephant," he wrote. Pilots have always been a superstitious lot, and the sight alarmed him. "Damn! . . . Jimmy shouldn't have forgotten old Tarfu. That little fella is good luck." Pottschmidt shrugged it off, suggesting Tarfu was looking out for himself, not his boss.

In Genovese's 1945 book, *We Flew without Guns*, he wrote that another CNAC pilot, Robbie Robertson, landed about two hours later with his cargo of U.S. Army officers and a few Chinese. The weather was too bad for the army but normal for CNAC. He reported that he had heard from Dean an hour or so earlier and that Dean was taking on a big load of ice up north. Robertson said he sounded worried. Robertson had flown farther south over Tali and had seen no Japanese, which he passed on to Dean.[1]

At the same time, some of the villagers at the bottom of Mount Dali (now Cangshan) heard a strange noise, almost like an explosion, on the mountain. Then they saw black smoke rising slowly from its crest. After puzzling over its meaning, they returned to their busy lives. Strange events on the mountain were far from unusual.

Genovese wrote after the war, "I carried little old Tarfu with me every time I flew after that. I thought it might bring me luck in finding Jimmy and his plane. But the weather was so bad we never got a glimpse of the ground on either the southern or northern route for almost two weeks, and by then the plane and the men in it must have been deep under the mountain snow. The search, carried on for many weeks on every occasion when we could see the ground, never revealed anything of the plane or its occupants."

I talked to Genovese several times before his death, and he sounded rather sad. He had no family, was then ninety-eight and living alone. He said he had kept Tarfu with him all through the years and had no one to give him to, so he asked if I would take him. I was ecstatic and told him I would take good care of the little guy. Weeks later a package arrived from Gen, and when I opened it I found, not a stuffed elephant, but a reasonably new penguin with the tag "Sea World Gifts" on it. It was not the good luck token that he had carried, that was obvious, but it was certainly nice of him to send its replacement.

Since the fliers were not members of any military service their MIA cases were handled by the U.S. State Department. Search-and-rescue units were formed some months later as newly organized the Search and Rescue Squadrons of the U.S. Army Air Corps (USAAC), but in late 1942, this function was handled by simple observation from normal flights. As Genovese recalled, there was never any sighting of CNAC No. 60 or its crew.

In later months, recognizing the perils of Hump flights, these search-and-rescue squadrons performed minor miracles, even parachuting specialists into downed aircraft when there was evidence of survivors. These units took their share of casualties as they went about their work, but the lift it gave to Hump pilots was significant. As the seasons changed, weather worsened and made the risks even greater. Search-and-rescue pilots were heroes for their dedication to their fellow airmen.

In one sense, the search for Jimmie, Dean, Yang, and CNAC No. 60 began the minute the plane was reported overdue. Other flights on similar routes were alerted to look for the downed C-47, and there were not that many downed aircraft in November 1942. Unfortunately, only a few weeks later the snow fell in the high country of the Himalayas and wreckage was soon just part of the rugged landscape. By the spring of 1943 there were far more planes to look for, even though there were more units specializing in spotting, then rescuing, lost crews.

As in most cases, the wreckage that was of interest was the wreckage that might house survivors. In the early days of Hump flying, few crews walked out of crashed airplanes. Survival had to be miraculous due to the jungle on one side of the flight and the towering peaks that followed. Many times, later in the war, local villagers were instrumental in attempting to save crash victims, sometimes successfully, sometimes not. However, in most cases those who survived Hump crashes did so thanks to miracles of timing, location, or circumstances—but there were few miracles, and none for CNAC No. 60.

On June 17, 1943, six months after the crash, the U.S. State Department issued death certificates for both Dean and Jimmie. These stated that the men had been missing for more than six months and were presumed dead. That conclusion was officially stated in "Report of the Death of an American Citizen," a U.S. State Department document dated June 17, 1943. Jimmie's family was traumatized by his death. They received $10,000 from CNAC as the agreed-upon death coverage, but they never recovered from his death. The Brownes had lost their only son. Yet they always hoped that someday Jim would walk through the front door and ask what was for dinner. That was a sad way to spend their last years.

In 2010 my wife, Donna, and I went on a trip to China with CNAC Association members. Angie Chen, a CNAC member who lives in Guangzhou, introduced us to a young Chinese author, Liu Xiatong, who had written a book titled *Flying the Hump*, and she wanted me to exchange my book *Airline at War* with him. His book was in Chinese, but Angie pointed out that in one of the chapters, in English, were the names James S. Browne and John J. Dean. That got my attention, and we happily swapped books.

Angie then gave me her translation of the Chinese character that surrounded those two names. Later I had several other translations that differed somewhat, but the gist was that the young author had discovered two radio transmissions from CNAC No. 60 in one of the old radio shacks that were part of the primitive navigational system used to cross the Hump. The translations indicated that two messages had been sent from the flight, one indicating all was normal and they were approaching the Himalayan range of mountains. The second message was far from a normal position report. It tersely reported that weather had suddenly worsened and that they were dumping their tin cargo to try to stay in the air. After that there was silence. And they had not even reached the Hump; they were just coming into the foothills of the Himalayas. But they would go no further.

# 7

## The Hump

The Hump routes over the Himalayas were probably the most dangerous routes anywhere. It is doubtful that Captain Sweet gave a complete description of the job ahead as Jimmie moved toward Dinjan.

Just how the routes into China from India came to be dubbed "the Hump" is anyone's guess. Probably a weary pilot climbing out of his c-47 after an adventurous crossing of the Himalayas called it that, and it stuck. During World War II it became the all-encompassing term for the many air routes crossing from India into China and vice versa. Descriptive as it was, the name caught on and became part of the vernacular.

In William M. Leary's book *The Dragon's Wings*, he quoted Bond's thoughts on air-supplying China in the event of war:

> There are many difficulties connected with this route [the Hump] of course. The country between Myitkyina and Yunanyi is high and rugged and the country west and north of this route, where the freight planes would be frequently forced to fly during air raids, is even worse. The weather is usually bad and the country is notoriously windy. Winds of forty to seventy miles per hour prevail most of the year. In clear weather flights would have to be at altitudes of from twelve thousand to fourteen thousand feet. To the west and north of course, but within seeing distance or . . . about one hundred miles, are peaks and

ranges more than seventeen thousand feet in height. However, we believe that with the proper exercise of care and training, all of these hazards can be controlled and once they have been controlled they in fact become safety factors, as the Japanese planes are not likely to go very far after our planes over that country in that weather.[1]

CNAC pioneered the first real attempts to mark a route over the rugged Himalayan range. In mid-1941 routes had been common from Lashio, Burma, to Kunming, connecting the narrow-gauge railroad running from Rangoon to Lashio, and then on to Kunming by road. Other routes had gradually closed or been too inefficient, plus the creeping Japanese forces had shut off French Indochina after the French consented to their presence. Added to that was the concern that Burma's future was very much in doubt, so bases in Lashio and Myitkyina would not be available.

On November 22, 1941, a CNAC DC-3 set out to plot a course from northern Assam, India, to Kunming. Capt. Chuck Sharp was the pilot, the copilot was Syd DeKantzow, and Joe Loh as the crew. Aboard were Bond and Arthur N. Young, a member of CNAC's Board of Directors. They began the flight in Lashio, flew over the new, almost completed Myitkyina airport, and on to Dinjan, a newly constructed field to be used by the RAF.

From Rangoon there was a small railroad connection to Calcutta which included barge transport but did allow equipment to find its way to Dinjan. Using Dinjan as the survey's starting point, the flight went east across the flatlands and jungles of northern India and Burma until it hit the mountain ranges of the Himalayas and then over the twelve-thousand- to fourteen-thousand-feet Himalayan peaks. On this November flight, after leaving Dinjan, they crossed the Burmese border toward Fort Hertz, crossed into China near Chungtien, and landed at Likiang. From there it was a clear shot to Kunming and the successful conclusion of a first real Hump flight.[2]

Later, to avoid Japanese fighters, these routes moved north, where peaks were in excess of twenty thousand feet, no match for an early C-47 or DC-3. So the pilots found passes to avoid the peaks, but these were subject to the vagaries of updrafts, downdrafts, and gusts up to one hundred miles an hour.

CNAC's C-47 and DC-3s continued flights from Lashio and Myitkyina for several months after America entered the war, but the Japanese moved rapidly north in Burma, and by April both airports were lost to the Chinese. From then on there would be flights from India into China from new bases springing up in Assam, including in Dinjan, Chabua, Jorhat, and Mohanbari.

CNAC pioneered the effort and was offering frequent flights in early 1942, but the U.S. Army Air Corps took its time to override the views of General Bissell, who consistently opposed any flights over the Himalayas. However, after President Franklin Roosevelt declared it critical to the war, the USAAC began a massive buildup of planes, airfields, and men to achieve the first ever air lifeline designed to support an entire nation.[3]

In 1941, as the war began, the U.S. Army Air Corps was still just that, a part of the army. It would not become a separate arm of the service until 1948. It had very limited experience in transporting and supplying troops with a need for speed and aircraft. Most troop movements, as were all mine in 1946 and 1951, were by sea in slow and uncomfortable ships. Most early and midwar movements from one theater to another were done with ships since the navy was used to moving people around, sometimes in elegance, sometimes not. But moving large quantities of equipment and supplies over territory not equipped with roads became the job of the air corps. It also became the supplier of all goods and services in far-flung outposts and garrisons.

As the war developed, troops needed to move to distant shores and be sustained there. Ships took too long to cross large bodies of water, so there became an almost immediate need for an air transportation system. As our fronts expanded and our troops multiplied, so did our need for a transport system.

Gen. William H. Tunner, later commander of the solution to this need, the Air Transport Command, was in at the very beginning. He writes in his book *Over the Hump* about his early years in air transport. He believed the creation of a transport unit stemmed from Roosevelt himself, who dictated a memo on May 28, 1941, to

Secretary of War Henry L. Stimson "suggesting" that the delivery of lend-lease aircraft destined for Britain be speeded up.[4] Thus was born the first Ferrying Command, led by Col. Robert Olds and supported by Tunner and one other captain. The Ferrying Command grew faster than most units, solving multitudes of logistical problems as they developed a vast network of routes used for American planes to be sent to various field commands.

The characteristics of a transport pilot were the same as those that Jimmie found in England. They were not heroes; they were to safely deliver their aircraft regardless of conditions. Ferry Command pilots learned the lesson the British had taught Jim: safety.

Still, the need for transports grew, so USAAC gave priority to the Ferry Command and it expanded even faster. Finally, it was decided to have a completely new arm of the air corps called the Ferry Command. Formed in April 1942 it was a tribute to the ingenuity, sweat, and dedication of men such as General Tunner that such a new and different type of air arm could be established in less than a year. In June the Ferry Command became the Air Transport Command (ATC). Then, recognizing the need for even more skills necessary to fly the Hump, the entire Hump airlift came under the ATC on December 1, 1942, just two weeks after Jimmie died on that dreaded Hump.

In the beginning there were two routes between Kunming and Dinjan, referred to simply as the southern via Yunnan Yi and the northern via Fort Hertz. By the war's end a chart of Hump routes numbered more than a dozen, with Easy, the southernmost, and Able, the northernmost. There were also routes that went to Chungking and to the various USAAC bases in India, showing times and headings. There was King, Roger, Love, and Charlie, all developed over four years of experimenting and plotting. Radio transmission stations sprang up to monitor these routes, all of which helped the pilots and crews, but all of which failed frequently or, with inexperienced operators, unknowingly pointed aircraft in the wrong direction.

Jim and John Dean's crash and their deaths were the first CNAC deaths on the Hump. One other DC-3, an army plane, had crashed in September 1942, killing its two pilots, apparently the first lives the Hump would take, but deaths would follow soon after Jim's.

That fact in itself led to new problems. Up until the CNAC No. 60 loss there had been no such thing as a "missing" flight. Most earlier fatal crashes had been located and bodies removed, but CNAC No. 60 had no protocol to convert "missing" to "dead." That became obvious in State Department correspondence with CNAC when each organization prompted the other to set up a determination of death. Eventually, after involving even the Indian government, they followed Bond's suggestion that after six months in a missing status, fliers would be legally classified as "dead, body not recovered."

What was it that made the Hump so dangerous? Start with the Himalayas, the world's tallest mountain range, and the weather system it creates. Updrafts and downdrafts of hundreds of feet per minute were unpredictable and deadly. On one occasion, several CNAC pilots had brought their loads of gas to Kunming and were getting ready to head back to Dinjan. Pete Goutiere wrote in his book, *Himalayan Rogue*:

On this particular day [March 11, 1943] one of the pilots said he knew a route through the mountains, where you didn't have to climb more than 10,000–12,000 feet to get through. If we followed him he would show us the way. His name was Pilot Welsh [Orin Welch]; his dad once built some small aircraft named after him. There was Sharkey in one plane, Jim Fox in ship 53, that I had first flown; Welsh, Sharkey, Fox, Johnson [Russell] and I. It was easy going right past Yunani, at 10,000 feet. We skirted Paoshan and Sugar Loaf Tali Mountain. We crossed the Mekong River. A bit bumpy and though I was flying, I was able to take a few pictures of the three planes in formation ahead of us. We crossed the next ridge, to see the Blue River below. Up ahead I saw Welsh head for what looked like a deep cut pass, gunsight shape, with Sharkey right on his tail. I could see clouds and mist coming over the mountains, then snow pelting the windshield. I kept my eyes on Sharkey, since Welsh had gone through and Sharkey was entering the gap. Fox was no more than 500–700 feet in front of us. The snow was blinding; I could barely see Fox's plane. I was losing the pass. Then

I saw Jim Fox's left wing catch a tree, he cartwheeled in a cloud of snow. I looked at my airspeed, it was down to 90 miles an hour. The vertical indicator showed I was going down at least 500 feet a minute. I hit the power and mixtures forward, stuck the nose down with a right turn. The pass is formed by two ledges at the hill that traverse straight down the pass to the river. I found myself in this gulch, easing the plane along as though I was hedgehopping downhill. I saw the airspeed building up but very slowly. I was praying that Jim Fox was okay. Oh, my God, I was sure he wasn't.[5]

Goutiere was right. Jim Fox died in that crash, but his story doesn't end there. His DC-3 No. 53 was lovingly taken down the mountain by nearby Pianma villagers and patched together. It sits in a little museum almost on the Chinese-Burma border.

In spite of the villagers' efforts they were unable to keep the right wing and landing gear, which wound up on the front lawn of the Kunming Walmart. But the reassembly of the rest of the airplane was done with great effort, without many of the sophisticated methods used in some other restorations. Its primitive, patched-up exterior speaks of the labors done by these unskilled but dedicated locals.

CNAC pilot Fletcher Hanks, a close friend of Fox's, tried to reach the plane in 1944 but failed. He tried again when he was in his eighties and eventually, with some help, made it to the wreck in June 1997. To show their respect for Fox, the Chinese presented his bust to the George H. W. Bush Presidential Library at Texas A&M University in June 2003.

Ironically, Orin Welch, who survived that day, was killed just two days after Fox, on March 13, 1943. He too was flying a C-53 between Fort Hertz and Dinjan and was hit by enormous updrafts and downdrafts; the theory was that his load of tin ingots bound for Dinjan broke free of their tie-downs and crashed through the floor, severing all control cables. Weather killed fliers, just as Japanese gunfire killed fliers.

The peaks and passes of the mountain ranges were full of danger, but flying over the Burma jungles was equally uninviting. Planes that went down in jungle areas left little chance of survival, given the denseness and loss of any sense of direction. Some crews did survive, but the hazards were many and the survival skills were not considered essential or even trainable in the first months. There was one case where a crew, or part of a crew, made it out after an incredible journey lasting forty-seven days.

On April 7, 1943, less than a month after the loss of Fox and Welch, CNAC's Joe Rosbert and Ridge Hammill, on his first Hump flight, took off from Dinjan headed for Kunming via Fort Hertz with a load of medical supplies. Weather was bad, with low temperatures at the higher elevations, making for another Hump danger: icing. Ice formed so rapidly on Rosbert's plane as soon as they got to sixteen thousand feet that it was a good five inches thick on the windshield, and blinded them. As more ice formed on the wings they began to lose altitude, and it became obvious that, with mountain peaks all around, they needed to turn back to Dinjan. The winds were stronger than they realized, and then Rosbert cried out, "My God, there's a mountain!"

In the crash, radio operator Wong died on impact. After the noise of the crash, the two who remained tried to get used to the total silence. An inventory told them they both suffered ankle and leg injuries and cuts and bruises. The snow and the wind were causing nearly hypothermic temperatures, so they wrapped themselves in parachutes and waited. There was no sleep, only snow for water, and one large bottle of cola syrup. After seven days they started out, broken limbs and all, tobogganing down the slopes until they lost their ride and continued sliding on their butts. They found a nearby hut with a warm fire, frightened children, and two old blind women. The women and children were scared, not sure of what to do, but saw a need for food on the faces of the battered pilots and cooked up some almost tasty mush. The dish had its effect on the two Americans. Rosbert, in his creative book, *Flying Tiger Joe's Adventure Story Cookbook*, mentioned, "Incidentally, those two 'dishes' proved to be the extent of their cuisine. After four days of such a diet, we had our first bowel movement in almost three weeks. That started my belief in a high fiber diet."

Their hosts, the Mishmis, a local tribe, moved them from hut to distant hut until they were greeted by a little man named Ah

Shaw, who grabbed a note from Rosbert and raced off into the forest. A little put out by his actions, they were relieved when he came back with four eggs and a telegram from a British camp some miles away. The only way to get from one location to another was by walking, and the broken ankles of both men, particularly Rosbert, were taking a terrible beating.[6]

At last, after forty-seven days, Rosbert and Hammill were reunited with their Dinjan friends and then flown to Calcutta, to the hospital there. Rosbert was sent back to the States for treatment of his overworked ankle and Hammill rested up before trying his second Hump flight. He crossed the Hump some four hundred times before, on May 5, 1945, only a few months before the war ended, he was flying without a radio operator and with a novice Chinese copilot. When he left the cockpit to set the radio frequencies, an engine died, and the copilot didn't know what to do. The plane went into a spin and centrifugal force pinned Hammill to the wall as the C-47 spun in.

So it was the topography and the weather that were the primary killers, but they were assisted by the lack of reliable ground-to-air communication. Primitive radio beacons guided them when everything went right, but these often failed, either by accident or by force of nature. Once, the Chinese moved a radio beacon some three hundred yards but never notified CNAC or ATC that there had been a change. As a result, Al Wright, a former AVG wingman, his copilot Charles Cook, M. K. Loh, and four Chinese boys paid the price.

Hump literature contains so many stories of impossible events and flights that no volume can tell them all. One relates the story of Capt. Glen Carroll, who became lost on a return to Dinjan on March 11, 1944, on a night with a low, solid overcast. High winds had driven him past the radio beacons and he had no visual check of ground features; as darkness fell and the gas gauges bounced on empty, he grew desperate. He later wrote in the CNAC publication *Wings over Asia*, "Flying at night, on top of a thick smoke-haze layer, with unknown ground speed, unknown wind and no navigational aids, our only chance was to hold to our course and hope for a break." Suddenly his copilot spotted the reflection from a river, and Carroll made a quick 180-degree turn to drop below the overcast and check for a possible ditching. With no time to spare he descended to the river and, wheels up, touched down on the water, skidding onto a sandbar; his left wheel well slid up on the bar so the ship turned 90 degrees, with the front section well out of the water. Later Carroll learned it was the Manas River that provided his landing strip.

It took three days for the crew to reach friendly forces; on the fourth day they found natives who guided them to the Indian town of Sorbhog, where they were subsequently taken to a road and picked up the British and eventually flown to Dinjan. There was much discussion about the condition of the downed c-47. Planes were in critically short supply, so heroic efforts were made to save any possible aircraft. Eventually it was decided that a party would be sent to the site to determine whether, and how, the DC-3 could be fixed.

The next day the party started out, trekking a mile above the wreck and floating down the river in a flimsy, bobbing raft with Art Prendergast and several Chinese mechanics. Just before they sighted the plane, a big bounce dumped one of the mechanics, named Wong, into the river. Almost immediately he was in trouble, for a crocodile found him after he hit the water. Fletcher Hanks described the scene in his book, *Saga of CNAC #53*: the other mechanics and Prendergast "had to watch helplessly as the crocodile thrashed Wong to death with the mechanic's screwdriver and pliers thrown in the air in the ensuing struggle. The croc swam off with Wong unconscious and bleeding and the other crocs rushed in to fight for a share of the food. They pulled Wong apart with a rolling, twisting motion."[7]

When they arrived at the site, sobered and sickened by Wong's death, they discovered that the plane could be salvaged and began their preparations. The task was far from simple; they needed the help of about twenty-five local natives and two of their best elephants, who dragged the plane to the river bank, helped load the engine and other parts into it, moved large rocks into place for a runway, and tamped the stones smooth with their giant feet.

Crocs were still a problem; when one attacked a local man, all the other men, armed only with sharp sticks, turned the beast away, wounded, their spears sticking in his mouth. Fletcher said, "The crocs spent all day eating their leader."

Soon work was finished, and the C-47, CNAC No. 81, was ready to fly again. Senior pilot Bill McDonald, who had come from Dinjan to coax the craft into the air, gave the scene his close attention. Hanks wrote that McDonald paced the length of the runway and inspected almost every stone; he suggested building a greater upsweep to give a little bit of a launch, and he placed marker stones at the 100-foot, 350-foot, and 500-foot points on the 700-foot runway. Yet in McDonald's description in a later book, *The Shadow Tiger*, written by his son William III,, he wrote, "On pacing the improvised runway we found it was only 150 feet long."[8] A rather significant difference, but with McDonald's masterful take-off and Prendergast as copilot and only fifty gallons of gas, the old transport lunged off the riverbank, skimmed the surface of the crocodile-infested river, and returned to duty flying the Hump.

This was a stunning example of a precision landing in bad weather, on an impossible landing spot, with repairs under the most primitive and dangerous conditions, and a superb pilot lifting the seventeen-thousand-pound plane, stripped of everything, off its elephant-crafted runway.[9] I wondered if Jim could be watching such events from above, yearning to be a part of such incredible scenes.

The rugged mountain peaks, the jungles, and the weather were certainly significant factors in the deadly Hump arena. But there was another factor, too, that compounded the problem: the Japanese fighters based at Myitkyina, barely three hundred miles from Kunming. The principal Japanese fighter was the Ki-27, with a range of 1,200 miles and an almost perfect record against the Chinese Air Force until the P-40s of the AVG arrived.

Although the lumbering old transports seemed a likely target, there is only one report of a CNAC plane lost to fighters. However, several others are still missing, with no knowledge of their final moments. On October 13, 1943, Marshall "Mike" Schroeder was coming home to Dinjan, flying high on a clear day, with several army transports when they were attacked and shot down. Goutiere said he had cautioned Schroeder about flying in clear weather with so many Japanese around.

While the Hump planes lost few of their number to the Japanese, their presence caused the routes on most flights to shift north, into higher peaks and rougher weather, and that too caused losses. In fact many CNAC and ATC planes were simply unaccounted for. Whether they were victims of weather, mountain peaks, mechanical failure, or the Japanese, it made little difference to the fate of the crews involved. In Jimmie's case, there is no way to tell whether he was a victim of Japanese guns or weather, engine problems or mountain peaks, yet our government cannot see its way clear to offer a combat award to him or his fellow crewmen.

There were more dangers, built into the very aircraft they flew. The C-47 was not a comfortable aircraft, with facilities known to modern aircraft. It had a primitive toilet in the rear that required the pilot to leave the cockpit, sometimes for extended periods. Often the copilots were inexperienced and unable to handle emergencies that frequently happened in flight. An engine missing its beat, the appearance of an unexpected peak, the shifting of cargo— all required immediate action. With the pilot otherwise occupied, danger was close at hand. At times the airborne problems were compounded by intestinal scizures that were hard to ignore. In one case, a pilot with the inevitable "trots" simply moved the toilet into the cockpit, to the horror of the rest of the crew.

Heating was another problem, as well as pressurization. Many of the flights took off from hot, humid Dinjan, and the crew had to adjust to the drastic temperature changes by adding layers of clothing. They would start out bare-chested and wearing shorts, then gradually add layers until they had donned their fur-lined jackets needed for subzero temperatures at altitude, temperatures that were beyond the limited capacity of early heaters. Oxygen was provided only for the crew, and even that had to be shared if the flight was extended for any reason. Neither of these problems seems major, but they were distractions for the crew when absolute vigilance was needed for most of the routes. The most significant concern was the mountains themselves, which created huge air movements that occurred without warning and could crush an airplane.

As the army's Air Transport Command expended and began to carry the bulk of cargo over the Hump, they lost large numbers of their relatively limited supply of aircraft, leaving what later would be called "the Aluminum Trail." It was said that a pilot could navigate from Assam to Kunming simply by tracking the wreckage of earlier flights. A pretty somber way to find your way. Years later Chick Marrs Quinn, the widow of a Hump pilot, compiled a list of 696 fatal wrecks that occurred in the China-Burma-India theater, incorporating as much data as she could find from information available in the Missing Air Crew Reports required by mid-1943. Her book, aptly named *The Aluminum Trail*, is a virtual encyclopedia of China-Burma-India air losses.

The Hump's name stuck, but its reputation only got worse. This was the world that confronted the American and Chinese crews as they tackled their daily runs. While CNAC No. 60's crew may have been early victims of the unknown perils of Hump flight, others would soon follow to create the tragic Aluminum Trail. CNAC was not spared in coming months: Jim Fox was lost on March 11, Orin Welch on the 13th, Sam Anglin in August. And the list continued to grow.

# 8

## The Crew

Jimmie was the copilot of CNAC No. 60, and his captain on their Kunming round-trip was John Joseph Dean of St. Peter, Minnesota. Born December 22, 1916, he was killed just prior to his twenty-sixth birthday in CNAC No. 60's fatal crash November 17, 1942. He left his new wife, Bess, in St. Peter; they had no children. John was the oldest of three children with a wide spread in ages. Robert was born in 1923, and much later, in 1931, Roy arrived, so there were fifteen years between John and Roy. Roy still remembers the days with John in Minnesota, when John doted on his tiny brother in the short visits and brief stays at their home: "When he disciplined me I was devastated, and even if my father told me, for example, that I didn't have to lie on the floor anymore for punishment, I would do nothing until John told me my punishment was at an end." Roy described John as tall, thin, and handsome. "He was my hero."

John went to the local high school, graduating in 1934. He briefly attended Gustavus Adolphus, a local college, and then attended the University of Minnesota in Minneapolis–St. Paul for three years. He went west to Kalispell, Montana, to learn to fly with the Jellison Flying Service. First they required him to master the skills of a mechanic, since plane repairs and maintenance usually fell to the pilot. He would have begun his aviation career in their little biplane Travelaire or their high-wing Monocoupe.

He left Kalispell for Seattle after his flight training and landed a job with Boeing. On a visit home he took brother Roy up for a ride in a rented open-cockpit at the airport in Mankato, Minnesota, and had just a little trouble avoiding electric lines as he landed. "I threw up as soon as we touched down," Roy admitted.

The navy seemed to appeal to fliers. The Depression was still a factor, and jobs were scarce, so John enlisted in July 1940 as a naval cadet. He had briefly been in the United States Naval Reserve, from October 13 to December 22, 1939, but came back for flight training in 1940. Assigned to Pensacola, he received his wings and his commission as an ensign, flying little pursuit planes. He was assigned to Fighting Squadron Three on the famed uss *Saratoga*, one of the early carriers originally designed to be a cruiser. The old carrier won the affection of her crew during its storied Pacific Ocean battles; battered and almost sunk on two occasions, it finally ended the war as an aviation classroom. After surviving all the actions of World War II, the gallant carrier went to the bottom as a result of nuclear testing in the Marshall Islands in 1946.

On the *Saratoga* and in San Diego John trained in the various aircraft required by naval warfare, such as the fighter F2A2, the F4F3, the Torpedo Bombers, and the Scout Bomber SBC4. Training included formation flying, dive bombing, navigation, gunnery, and instrument flying. On a leave from the navy, John went home to St. Peter, looking, according to his brother, very dapper in spats. He was, for unknown reasons, the grand marshal of St. Peter's 4th of July Parade in 1941.

In the summer of 1941 his naval base was visited by several men representing the American Volunteer Group, later to be known as the Flying Tigers. Pilots and mechanics were offered fabulous opportunities flying for the Republic of China and fighting the Japanese. While the U.S. was not yet involved in the war, there was some sentiment against the Japanese for its brutal occupation of China, and the AVG offer was a chance to make great money and get in the fight. Flight leaders would be paid $650 a month, and wingmen $600. Compared to the average monthly paycheck of navy aviators of about $210 per month, that was fantastic money. And they would get $500 for every Japanese plane shot down.[1]

President Roosevelt had given the volunteers permission to resign from the service in order to sign a one-year contract with the AVG. And, although it was never specified in the contract but was implied by recruiters, the volunteers would be allowed to return to their service after their contract was up and receive credit for their year away. As an added bonus they would fly the new P-40, a big improvement over the navy's fighters. The decision was an easy one for John; in September 1941 he resigned his commission and signed a one-year contract with the American Volunteer Group, commanded by retired Army Air Corps captain Claire Chennault, one of the most famous fighting teams ever put together. (His contract was actually with an entity called "Central Aircraft Manufacturing Company"; because government officials wanted the AVG to be a secret, they devised dummy companies and elaborate cover-ups to hide the airmen's journey to the Pacific. The first contingent arrived on the West Coast in July 1941, with passports describing them as plumbers, clerks, artists, and other occupations that had no relation to the passport bearer.)

First, though, John was allowed to go home for a last visit. While there he married his high school sweetheart, Bess Klein, and told her of the fabulous opportunity he had in China. She was a local girl whose father owned a furniture store and mortuary enterprise. Young brother Roy was an altar boy at the wedding, charged with the responsibility of protecting the honeymooners' luggage. Still awed by his older brother, he remembered, "I fought like a tiger (blows even) when our uncle-in-law tried to put rice in the luggage." Possibly as part of the wedding celebration, John took his father's car out one evening. The next morning, Roy saw the car with its top was caved in; it had obviously been rolled, but then must have righted itself. John had driven it home, parked it in the garage, and gone to bed. "I do not remember hearing any explanation," Roy wrote.

John sailed from California on the transport *Boschfontein*, landing in Rangoon with his phony passport on November 12, 1941, with twenty-five other pilots. In the next few weeks, new pilot Eric Shilling and others convinced the colonel to paint the newly assembled P-40 Warhawks with the now famous shark mouth that identified the group. On November 25, 1941, John was assigned to the 1st Squadron, later to be known as the Adam and Eves, as a wingman, with Sandy Sandell as his squadron leader; they were located at Kyedaw Airfield near Toungoo in Burma.

But the game changed on December 8, when Japan attacked Pearl Harbor, Wake, Guam, Hong Kong, Manila, and other Far East cities. Chennault then had to juggle his meager resources, so he ordered one squadron, the 3rd, to Rangoon's Mingaladon Airfield and in December sent the rest of the group to Kunming.

On the way there John had a problem. Flying at twenty-one thousand feet his oxygen tube came loose and he passed out. As he drifted to lower altitude, he regained consciousness and climbed back into formation. However, with Himalayan peaks rising to twenty-one thousand feet, slipping into lower altitudes was risky. He was happy to sight Kunming airport, although as the squadron approached they saw the havoc wreaked by a recent Japanese air attack. After landing and heading to their billets, they were appalled to see stacks of dead Chinese in the streets. It was a sober welcome. Soon after their arrival several 1st Squadron members, including John, joined 3rd Squadron at Mingaladon Field for the defense of Rangoon, but he was sent back to Kunming on December 16 to rejoin the 1st Squadron.

On December 20 the AVG got its first taste of combat. A flight of Kawasaki Ki-48s was headed for Kunming to finish what they had begun on the 17th. The 2nd Squadron missed them, but the 1st Squadron ran straight into the bombers and in furious fighting downed over seven of them, though only four were confirmed. John found himself part of the melee and was credited with a share in the action, earning himself a bonus of $133.33.

For the next month aerial combat continued, with the Flying Tigers accumulating significant numbers of Japanese bombers and fighters. Twelve 1st Squadron ships had been sent back to Rangoon from Kunming on January 24, just in time for the next big show. John's next score was on January 29 back in Rangoon. Several flights of Japanese fighters headed for the Allied airfield and were intercepted by a mixed AVG and British group of planes. In the melee, AVG pilots were given credit for eleven downed Japanese, and John received credit for one air-to-air kill—a $500 present for Mrs. Dean. It also earned him his first citation from Colonel Chennault. Sadly, Louis Hoffman, who flew with him in the 1st Squadron, was killed in that fight.[2]

John's citation may have made up for a reprimand he had received just days after his second kill. On December 31 a photo reconnaissance mission was sent out, but apparently encountered problems. An investigation on January 15 cleared the pilots of any wrongdoing, but Chennault remarked for the record "that the entire flight was conducted in an amateurish manner unworthy of experienced pilots."

During the first months of 1942 rumors increased concerning the status of the AVG and the Army Air Corps. Since the United States was now in the war, it seemed inappropriate for Americans to fight as part of the Chinese Air Force, although their commander was Chennault. The rumors kept getting stronger until April 15, when Chennault was brought back into the Army Air Corps, then one week later promoted to brigadier general. That sparked a revolt among the pilots, who were already upset about flying ground support missions for the Chinese, which were very risky and not, they believed, among their duties. They believed they should be attacking Japanese aircraft. Chennault calmed them down by informing them that the AVG was to disband on July 4, 1942; the fate of the members had not been determined.

Things improved for John as the AVG neared its end. On May 11, 1942, he was promoted to flight leader, with a pay increase, and on June 12 the Adam and Eves, some in their new, improved P-40Es, the Kittyhawks, took on five bombers and eight fighters of the Japanese air forces in Nanking. After some hair-raising combat they downed nine planes; John accounted for two, a bomber and a fighter, earning Mrs. Dean another $1,000. His total kills now stood at 3.25. He also was decorated by the Chinese government with the Air Force 1 star Medal 6th Grade Cloud Banner Decoration.

As the AVG wound down, pilots and ground crews had to decide whether to be inducted in the USAAC, return to civilian life, or stay on in China and work for China National Aviation Corporation. John chose to fly with CNAC. He was offered a chance to go home before he began his service, but, according to Roy, he stayed in China instead.

Although John Dean's remains are on Cangshan, the website FindaGrave.com indicates that he has a headstone in Calvary Cemetery in St. Peter, Minnesota. It is a good size, a pretty marble stone, but seems lonely with only the name "Dean" inscribed on its face.[3]

The third crew member on Jimmie's fatal flight was the radio operator, whom CNAC recorded as K. L. Yang but later sources named Kuan Liu Young. He was the Chinese crew member who transmitted Dean's last urgent messages just before their crash. Little is known about Young, which is the case with most Chinese air crew members. While many records exist of the pilots, few are left to tell about the support group of Chinese. That is doubly sad because they were subjected to the same perils of the infamous Himalayan Hump flights. Records estimate that ninety-five Chinese crew members died flying for CNAC in World War II, compared to thirty-five pilots and copilots. It is important to remember Kuan Liu Young as the representative of all his other Chinese crewmen who perished with their American pilots.

Another element of unfairness toward the Chinese was the matter of pay. It was originally determined by CNAC that there would be two pay scales for flight personnel, one for Caucasian pilots and the other for Chinese pilots and copilots. This was further complicated by the fact that a number of flight personnel were of Chinese extraction but had trained and were living in Canada and the U.S. These men were also subjected to the lower pay scale in a move that became increasingly irritating as the wartime risk was equal for all flying staff.

Some of the crew members who were most unhappy with the pay inequities found ways to make up the difference. Tommy Wing, a native of Chicago, joined CNAC in late 1944 and was made a captain after his brief stint as a copilot. He took great exception to the pay differences, as did others, and decided to make up the difference by smuggling cigarettes into China. He was successful for a period, but eventually he was discovered and was fired by

Managing Director Bond. This was shortly after the war ended, when some competition with CNAC had begun. Wing's response to his dismissal was to walk across the street and be immediately hired by Central Air Transport Company, a new airline that was cofounded by another disgruntled Chinese CNAC pilot, Moon Chin.

Sadly, a short time later Wing was killed when his plane crashed in one of commercial aviation's worst days, Christmas 1946. Two CNAC planes went down in zero-zero weather over Shanghai's Lunghwa airport, and Wing's crashed in a nearby airport. One CNAC plane made it safely, but pilot Joe Michiels couldn't remember if he even saw the runway before his wheels touched the ground. He was an early survivor of a primitive instrument landing system, recently installed at nearby Kian Gwan airport.

**1.** Tiro Vorster, painting of a C-47 take-off in
bad weather, 1999. Courtesy of Tiro Vorster.

**2.** Jimmie Browne at age eight, 1929.
Courtesy of Joseph Rushton and Evelyn A. Kaht.

**3.** Jimmie with his father, Herbert Browne, 1929.
Courtesy of Joseph Rushton and Evelyn A. Kaht.

**4.** Jim's graduation picture
in the Riverside Military
Academy yearbook, 1940.
Courtesy of Riverside
Military Academy,
Gainsville, Georgia.

**5.** The Chung, China National
Aviation Corporation's symbol,
undated. Courtesy of CNAC.org.

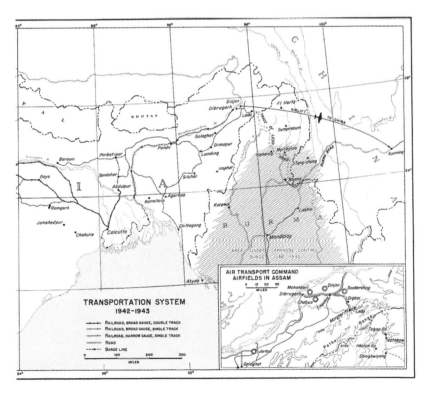

**6.** Chine-Burma-India transport network,
1942–43. Courtesy of www.ibiblio.org.

**7.** A CNAC C-47 in flight over the Himalayan Hump, 1945. Courtesy of Chris Bull.

**8.** John Joseph Dean, flight leader 1st Squadron, AVG, 1942. Courtesy of Roy Dean and Hunter Robbins Air Museum.

9. AVG P-40s in stack formation, 1942. Photo by
AVG pilot R. T. Smith. Courtesy Brad Smith.

10. CNAC No. 60 C-47 in flight, 1942.
Courtesy of CNAC.org.

**11.** Instrument panel and cockpit of a C-47, 1942. Courtesy of San Diego Air and Space Museum and Linda Burnley.

**12.** The author exchanging books with Liu Xiatong in Kunming, 2010.

**13.** CNAC Association group on Peninsula Hotel rooftop, Hong Kong, 2010.

**14.** Clayton Kuhles of MIA Recoveries, Inc. discussing plans for his climb with locals, 2011. Courtesy of MIA Recoveries, Inc.

**15.** Clayton Kuhles on Cangshan Mountain, 2011.
Courtesy of MIA Recoveries, Inc.

**16.** Campsite on Dali Mountain, 2011.
Courtesy of MIA Recoveries, Inc.

**17.** CNAC No. 60 crash site area, 2011. Courtesy of MIA Recoveries, Inc.

**18.** Construction number 4681 found on a piece of CNAC No. 60 wreckage, 2011.

**19.** Celebration of the seventieth anniversary of the end of World War II, Beijing, 2015.

**20.** Parade at the celebration of the seventieth anniversary of the end of World War II, Beijing, 2015.

**21.** The author and son at the celebration of the seventieth anniversary of the end of World War II, Beijing, 2015.

**22.** The author at 9,400 feet on Cangshan Mountain, 2015.

**23.** The view from 9,400 feet looking down on
Erhai Lake and the city of Dali, China, 2015.

**24.** Monument to the Aviator Martyrs in the War of
Resistance against Japanese Aggression, Nanjing, 2006.

**25.** Map of Hump area, 1945.

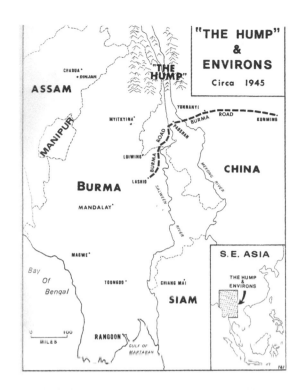

**26.** Saying goodbye to Fan Jianchuan at his museum, 2018.

**27.** Bust of Jimmie in the Square of the Chivalrous Friends of China, Jianchuan Museum, 2018.

**28.** Sun Chunlong and Angie Chen at the office of Shenzhen Longyue Charity Foundation, Kunming, 2018.

# 9

## The American Volunteer Group

While it is true that the American Volunteer Group as a whole played no part in Jimmie's life, the Flying Tigers did. The AVG had been blessed with the strange nickname, and that name would last long after the demise of the famous group of early volunteers. So it was to the new Flying Tigers, the Army Air Corps' 23rd Fighter Group, that Jimmie delivered his load of gas in Kunming on the morning of November 17, 1942. The 23rd had several AVG pilots and crewmen and was still bossed by the craggy Old Man of the AVG, Brig. Gen. Claire Chennault.

The AVG had begun in secrecy and stealth in mid-1941, as the word was put out that pilots were needed immediately to fight the Japanese airplanes decimating the coastal cities of China. It was a message that came directly, if not publicly, from President Franklin Roosevelt and in a short time resulted in one hundred pilots and a cadre of mechanics and support personnel. Among the pilots was the famous Greg Boyington, a Congressional Medal of Honor winner and, much later, a role model for the TV series *Black Sheep Squadron*. There were also two nurses and two doctors plus a dentist to look after the health of the daring young men.

They initially gathered in stages in San Francisco, claiming to be teachers, plumbers, salesmen, and a host of other professions that had nothing to do with aviation, hoping to keep their presence and their mission from the public. In that they were not successful.

The advance party of thirty left San Francisco on the *President Pierce* before the first contingent of pilots, nurses, and mechanics left on the *Jagersfontein* on July 8, 1941, escorted by the navy's *Salt Lake City* and *Northampton*. The contracting organization for the AVG was the Central Aircraft Manufacturing Company (CAMCO), which was responsible for getting these volunteers to China in one piece. In San Francisco they selected a leader for this adventuresome group, whose name was Joe Rosbert.[1]

The *Jagersfontein* stopped in Honolulu for three days, then continued on across the broad Pacific waters to Manila, where they passed the Bataan peninsula and the island of Corregidor, knowing nothing of their impending tragedies. Their arrival in Singapore on August 11 was welcome after six weeks on the Dutch ship. Rosbert thought he had completed his job, but he was not yet off the hook. First he had to pay off the bar bills of his thirsty volunteers, then he had to arrange transportation to Rangoon, where CAMCO would take over.

According to Rosbert's book, *Flying Joe's Adventure Story Cookbook*, he was fortunate enough to find a freighter, the *Tarakan*, to take his crew on to Burma. After two more stops along the way, they finally arrived in Rangoon on October 29, completing their exotic introduction to the Far East. Finally, Rosbert was relieved of his duties as group leader, much to his relief.

The last group of AVG airmen arrived on November 21, 1941, only two weeks before Pearl Harbor. These volunteers had pledged themselves to help China, not knowing that America would become involved in the war before the AVG fired its first shot.

So it was that the final forces of the American Volunteer Group were now assembled and organized into three squadrons. The 1st Squadron, under Sandy Sandell, was nicknamed the Adam and Eves. The 2nd Squadron, under Jack Newkirk, was named after the famous Chinese Panda Bear, and 3rd Squadron, led by Oley Olson, called themselves Hell's Angels.[2]

Their stay in Rangoon was brief. They were put on a train for their first destination, Toungoo, Burma, where their training and the war would start. Training was intensive, realistic, and deadly. In the first months of AVG's existence they lost three pilots—Max

Hammer, Peter Atkinson, and John Anderson—all due to accidents in the powerful P-40.[3]

The AVG was probably better prepared than most military units in the China-Burma-India theater. In the first week of the war after Pearl Harbor, Chennault made moves to use his squadrons most effectively. The RAF was pleading for help to support its 67th Squadron in the protection of Rangoon, so Chennault sent 3rd Squadron to Mingaladon airport outside Rangoon to join the RAF and their outdated Brewster Buffalos on December 11. Next, on December 17, 1st Squadron was sent by air and by the Burma Road to Kunming, where they would remain. And with their support people trucking over the nasty Burma Road, 2nd Squadron would follow the 1st to Kunming.

Combat soon followed, first in Kunming on December 20, and then in Rangoon a few days later. Results of those first encounters with the nimble Japanese fighters, the Nakajima K-27s, were very satisfactory, and the formations of bombers, principally the Mitsubishi Ki-21, failed to get much protection in the hour-long battle. According to Daniel Ford's *Flying Tigers*, the score was pretty one-sided, with AVG fliers reporting a number of downed Japanese bombers (four confirmed) but only one P-40 damaged and no pilot losses.

Heavier fighting was ahead for 3rd Squadron; on December 23 they fought a day-long battle with massed Japanese Mitsubishi K-21 bombers, loosely protected by fighters. In the air battles of December 23 and 25, according to the Headquarters First American Volunteer Group, the 3rd Squadron downed ten bombers and one fighter on the 23rd and twelve bombers and eight fighters on the 25th. While that was impressive, it was not without cost. Henry Gilbert and Neil Martin lost their aerial battles and died. The ratio was comforting, yet when you put names to the losses, the joy of victory dimmed.

In coming months the squadrons were shuffled to where they were needed most. Mingaladon was abandoned when the Japanese took Rangoon, and all forces concentrated in Kunming when Lashio, the Burma terminus, fell in April. During 1942, AVG squadrons were used for the usual air protection of cities, but also in bomber escort, strafing runs, and reconnaissance flights. In another unexpected benefit, the AVG raised U.S. morale, showing the first aggressive offensive action that ended successfully. The Japanese juggernaut had rolled over Asia and the Pacific, including its horrendous Pearl Harbor victory, leaving the nation stunned. But the Flying Tigers shone a bright light that led the way for future victories and eventual triumph.

These airmen combined to put on a wonderful show for the nation and for our Allies, but they were not a perfect bunch. Many left before the unit disbanded; at one point there was a mass request for termination of their contracts. They were often an unruly, undisciplined lot, but together they were more than impressive. So individual misbehavior, punishment, and misdeeds were mostly forgotten as the Chinese bestowed their praise and thanks on the survivors who had persevered until the end.

Since the U.S. Army did not take kindly to the idea of a separate air unit not under its control, the American Volunteer Group was officially terminated on July 4, 1942, and a new U.S. Army Air Corps unit, the 23rd Fighter Squadron, became the new Flying Tigers. While the name was transferred to the air corps unit, nothing would ever change the fact that the Flying Tigers were those who came before the sounds of Pearl Harbor and paved the way for the future. Chennault's records list 294 Japanese aircraft downed, although Ford's number is a little higher, 296. As is the American way, there was a score card. In Chennault's report to CAMCO on July 25, 1942, the pilots of the AVG were officially owed $146,999.87 for their aerial victories, to be divided among sixty-six pilots. John J. Dean was awarded $1,633.33. On the debit side, ten pilots and one crew chief died in action, and nine pilots died in noncombat accidents.[4]

# 10

## The Plane

The plane Jimmie and John Dean were flying was a well-tested workhorse of an airplane. Years later, Gen. Dwight D. Eisenhower called the C-47 one of the four most significant weapons in the winning of the war.

In reality, it was the military cargo version of the DC-3, a Douglas airplane that succeeded the DC-2, although their similarities were remarkable. The DC-2 was a very radical departure from the earlier aircraft of the 1920s and 1930s. The DC-3 was bigger than its predecessor, more powerful, and carried twenty-one passengers compared to the DC-2's fourteen. The DC-3 became known under a variety of numbers and names. First it was the DC-3, then the army modified it and reclassified it as a C-53, then further modifications were made, reinforcing the flooring, and widening the doors for ease in loading cargo.

The two former classifications were as a passenger transport, but the early C-47DL was designed to haul freight, and only occasionally people. It was named the Skytrain or the Skytrooper, but British versions were called Dakotas, while the navy, with little imagination, called them R4-Ds. In later wars their missions became more combat-related, carrying rapid-firing machine guns to support ground troops. During World War II they were the Gooney Birds.

CNAC found a place in its heart for the DC-2, and later the DC-3, beginning with the arrival of the first DC-2s in the spring of 1935.

Its sleek lines, relatively quiet cabin, and stability in the air made it a passenger's dream. Almost immediately the DC-2 became the airline workhorse.

The three routes then in existence were over some flatlands that provoked less turbulence than the wartime fliers would encounter over the Himalayas. But bad things happened to some of the DC-2s. On August 24, 1938, Capt. Hugh Woods did his usual precise preflight, loaded his crew and passengers on his DC-2, nicknamed the *Kweilin*, and with eighteen souls on board, climbed into the still hazy Hong Kong skies.

So far no CNAC planes had been attacked by the Japanese, but Japanese fighters and bombers had had no such reluctance to pound Chinese cities. The Sino-Japanese War had been going on for several months, so CNAC pilots were versed on what evasive action they could take if attacked, all CNAC planes being completely unarmed. August 24, 1938, would make the exception. As the DC-2 reached altitude, Woods saw eight Japanese float biplanes dead ahead and coming straight at him. There were no clouds to shield him, a usual tactic, and by now they had him in their sights. Bullets began pinging off the plane, tearing tiny holes in the fabric, so he made his decision: he lowered flaps, cut power, and headed for a river. His landing was perfect, right next to the bank so everyone could get out, but the current was too strong and pulled the plane out to the middle. By then, the Japanese planes were back, machinegunning the downed transport with wave after wave of vicious strafing. The plane was plainly marked as a transport, so there could be no miscommunication; it was a deliberate attack. And it was the first commercial airliner ever shot down by a hostile aircraft.

Woods was taken to safety with his other two survivors, a passenger and the radio operator, but fourteen crew and passengers lay dead on the river bank. Protests were filed with the Japanese, whose only response was that the attacking pilot had not been able to identify the silver liner as a civilian plane. Testimony from the three survivors made clear that it was an obvious attack on China and American nationals. But from Tokyo came only silence.

CNAC at this time was desperate for airplanes, so the battered *Kweilin* was resurrected from the muddy waters of the river and rebuilt by the talented lead mechanic, Zig Soldinski, and his Chinese crew. Given the condition of the waterlogged craft and the paucity of sophisticated tools, it was a miracle that the DC-2 ever flew again.

The restored aircraft had been back in service only a short time when pilot Walter "Foxie" Kent loaded his DC-2 with his crew of four to take care of his nine passengers. Then he lifted his plane off the Kai Tak runway at Hong Kong and headed for Kunming. He landed at an airfield near Suifu, and even with knowledge that Japanese planes were somewhere near Kunming he decided to chance it. He flew toward Kunming but, seeing planes still over the city, he circled behind the mountains to stay out of sight.

Risking running out of fuel, he finally had to do something, so he put down on Changyi field's short runway. It may have been his only move, but it was a bad decision, since five enemy pursuit planes were just leaving after strafing the Changyi field. They turned back as the liner rolled to a stop, and just as the wheels stopped rolling, the first shells hit the plane. Stewardess Lu Mei-ying did her best to get the passengers out and scattered, but lost her life performing her duties. Kent, shot through the head, died instantly. Three crew members died, as did six of nine passengers. It was another tragic event for the renamed, renumbered, and rebuilt *Kweilin*.

In spite of feelings in Washington that war could be averted, there was no such optimism in the Far East. A Eurasia plane also was shot down, so there was no confusion in anyone's mind that Japan was headed for war and was perfectly content to provoke incidents to show both their arrogance and their lack of concern toward nations near and far. And that was their major flaw.

The days of the DC-2 were numbered by the time war broke out, and it was replaced by an even better aircraft. Faster, roomier, and more economical, the DC-3 was a plane everyone wanted. Fortunately, the combination of Pan Am power and CNAC need was enough to get one, which went into service on November 17, 1939. DC-3s had been around in the States since 1935, but even four years later it was a welcome sight to the pilots of CNAC. The planes proved amazingly robust, as witnessed by the May 20, 1941, encounter with a flight of Japanese. Woods was again the pilot, but his aircraft was CNAC No. 46, one of the first DC-3s more or less finagled from the French. Thus began the previously told story of the DC-2½.

The C-47 was a modified version of the C-53. The major difference was that they were designed for cargo, not passengers. Flooring was reinforced and cargo doors were bigger so larger weapons and vehicles could be loaded, such as a 37mm gun or a new Jeep. In the case of CNAC flights, the larger doors were lifesavers when cargo had to be dumped, as often happened, to lighten the plane. Sometimes the planes were fitted with bucket seats along the sides to hold paratroopers, and sometimes other modifications were made to accommodate other configurations. It was a highly versatile aircraft.

Usually these planes carried a crew of three, although in China often just the pilot and radioman were on board. Oxygen was available only to the cockpit crew and was necessary when flying much above twelve thousand feet. Many of the Hump route peaks were well above that level, so passengers were exposed to oxygen deprivation, which caused extreme symptoms including death. And, of course, there were no parachutes for passengers.

There are a number of cases where pilots ordered their crews to bail out if the plane was in trouble, but if they were carrying passengers, the fliers would stay at their posts and do their best to save both lives and the plane. Few succeeded. One bomber pilot in India had wounded crew aboard, and after the unwounded had bailed out, the pilot stayed in his seat, knowing he could not clear the mountains ahead. He was awarded the Congressional Medal of Honor posthumously. It was the only Medal of Honor awarded in the China-Burma-India arena in the entire war.

CNAC No. 60 was a C-47DL Douglas Aircraft that had been flying for CNAC just a month. The plane was part of a lend-lease shipment of aircraft that provided CNAC with most of its planes during the war. The Lend-Lease Program had been used to keep Britain in the war with Germany when it was illegal for the U.S. to sell or give war goods to any combatant nation. President Roosevelt came up with the idea, knowing the state of Britain's finances and their desperate need for more military might. The original transaction involved a number of American destroyers, which were used by the British to fight the U-boat campaign. In recent months the number of nations benefiting from the arrangement included China, and war materials were coming in fast.

The first ten planes furnished were C-53s, the U.S. Army's version of the highly successful Douglas DC-3, converted to provide for military needs. From the DC-3 came the cargo version, called the C-47. It provided the backbone of material movement early on. In Britain it was the Dakota; in China it was the Skytrain; in the U.S. it was often called the Gooney Bird, but it was just a C-47.

Larry Davis's C-47 *Skytrain in Action* offers some interesting facts in the stages of the C-47. The DC-3 had been developed from a previous commercial design that was adapted for American Airlines. Its predecessor was a DC-2 that had been improved by Douglas to answer the need for a bigger and more adaptable version. That became the DST series, now considered the first DC-3. DST stood for Douglas Sleeper Transport, which had been designed for American Airlines. It provided sleeper berths for fourteen passengers or regular seating for twenty-eight. From that series of DST DC-3s came the first C-47s.

The designation C-47DL indicated that it was one of the early versions of the aircraft. It was reinforced for heavier, larger cargo and in some cases had ringbolts on the floor for strapping down cargo. Later versions, the C-47A and C-47B, were more powerful, but still carried the same dimensions as the C-47DL. However, at 17,865 pounds they were heavier, had higher ceilings of 26,400 feet, and had a combined authorized weight of 31,000 pounds. The C-47B was designed for Hump flights, having blowers to give more power at altitude.[1]

CNAC No. 60 was a low-wing monoplane with two 1,200 HP Pratt & Whitney radial engines and a ninety-five-foot wingspan and stood seventeen feet tall. It could reach a maximum of 230 miles per hour, but cruised at only 207. Its construction number was 4681 and its serial number was 41-18556. It was the first C-47 that CNAC received; all others coming from the U.S. had been C-53s. It also was reported to be the first plane to have a blower for additional power at altitude. One of the CNAC pilots, Fletcher

Hanks, told me that he was sure the new blower had exploded when initiated at altitude and the plane simply blew apart and would never be found. I did learn later that the first blowers were not installed until 1943.

Jimmie's plane was not pressurized and had a heater that was undependable and, even at its best, was not adequate for the freezing temperatures at higher altitudes. They frequently flew passengers, particularly Chinese soldiers, who were terrified before they took off and panicked easily in the air. Most Chinese soldiers had never flown before, and now were being flown over mountain ranges that developed updrafts or downdrafts which often would bounce the soldiers off the ceilings, then slam them to the deck. Safety belts had not been invented yet, but sometimes the men would rope themselves together in a hopeless gesture. Sadly, not all passengers survived a Hump flight. Since there was no oxygen for passengers, they sometimes passed out and often were sick. Longtime CNAC pilot Pete Goutiere told of one flight:

> They were a happy-go-lucky crowd, joking and teasing each other, sitting on bucket seats stretched along the sides of the C-47. There were no stewardesses or even seat belts, so before they boarded the plane, Goutiere marched the troop to the rear of the plane for a mandatory relief call. When they were all on board he took a long, stout rope and attached it through the seat belt anchors, tying the troops all together. Then they took off, peaking their altitude at 17,000 feet where it was rough and freezing cold, then dropped down to skim the fields in the hot humid air of the valley.
>
> During the four hour flight, Peter had not cracked open the cabin door, fearing what he might see. After landing he described the flight. "This trip the troops had been roasted, frozen, blacked out, roasted again, rough-aired again and then finally on the ground in a little less than four hours."[2]

The cabin's condition was an indication of the Chinese soldiers' displeasure, with vomit making the cabin floor as slick as an ice rink. When operated as their design intended, C-47s were the most useful plane, but comfort for passengers was not included in that design.

CNAC and its C-47s not only provided troop movements but also furnished supplies to ground troops on the ground. Later in the war CNAC would be asked to fly loaded with sacks of foods, rice mostly, at scary altitudes of two hundred feet or less. At a signal, and braced by the far wall of the plane, crew designated as "kickers" would shove the supplies out to smash into the ground seconds later. Most of the time it was Chinese who were kickers, but occasionally U.S. Army troops would be used. One of the more cynical ground noncoms told of an incident that supposedly happened on one such drop. He claimed that rough weather had shoved not only the supplies out of the plane, but the kicker as well. The noncom said it was no problem, though, because the kicker's replacement arrived seconds later, spread-eagled on a dropped rice bag. Stories could survive even when logic seemed to disprove the telling.

Originally CNAC No. 60 had been assigned to the 10th Air Force in India; that was on September 2, 1942. It went to the China Division on October 14, and subsequently to CNAC on October 18.[3] Less than a month later, in the fog and drizzle of November 17, having barely completed thirty days of wartime service, it buried itself in the side of Cangshan Mountain.

# PART 3

---

## THE SEARCH

# 11

## The Search Takes Shape

This was the world of the crew of CNAC No. 60. As my wife, Donna, and I continued our research for our several books, we kept probing for further information about CNAC, the Hump, aircrew casualties, and a host of other subjects. As our own books were completed, we concentrated more and more on the subject of Jim. But the years went by and we found few clues as to his fate. It dawned on me that the huge losses experienced on the Hump were by far the greatest for the U.S. Army Air Corps, not for CNAC; that encouraged us to believe that our search would be narrower than we first envisioned. We really had no plan to actually find Jim, only to know more about his world of aviation in war.

Our research began back in the 1960s, when we became hooked on the Civil War. We had found some letters in the attic of our cottage in Pentwater, Michigan, that dated back to the Civil War. They were from my great-grandfather Gordon Willett to his wife, Mary, while he was aboard a ship of the U.S. Sanitary Commission taking wounded from Jamestown, Virginia, to Washington in the 1860s. The letters were warm, personal, and very romantic, and they made the oval portraits in the dining room come alive. So we decided to focus on finding out what happened on just one day of the Civil War. That subsequently became a book, but early on it was more of a fascinating hobby, sometimes reluctantly involving our three youngsters.

One of our favorite sources and our most productive was the Library of Congress. But the process is not very efficient for the reader, since book retrieval from the vast collection of volumes takes time. We would put in a request for books, then wait twenty to thirty minutes for the volumes to show up on our desk. We spent the time viewing the card catalogue (since replaced by computer screens) to look for other sources.

CNAC became one of our targets, and there were several books devoted to the airline. In a sense, that marked the beginning of our search for the answers of Jim's disappearance. We found one clue in a book by Gen Genovese about Jim's last flight. There was a book by William Langhorne Bond, the airline's savior during its hectic lifetime, but little about the men of the airline. Although the search for Jimmie was a by-product of other research, our interest in his story grew slowly despite the scarcity of factual material.

Besides the Library of Congress, we had always found the National Archives and the U.S. Army Military History Institute in Carlisle, Pennsylvania, to be our most productive sources. But CNAC was a different case; it was a civilian airline, a partnership between the Republic of China and Pan Am, so federal depositories had little information on it. Then we discovered that Pan Am's collection of materials was in Coral Gables at the Richter Library of the University of Miami. It was a real gold-mine of information about CNAC as well as Pan Am and its other affiliates. The problem was that it was not indexed except in a very general way. The university was hoping to get funds to do a more refined index, but without that tool we simply had to go box to box. There were more than six hundred boxes, as I remember. Our first stint there lasted two weeks and we hated to leave. The staff were exceptionally helpful, and I had a little machine called a Star Writer, which is a typewriter with a printer, so we could get hard copy of pertinent items. Unfortunately the Star Writer's memory capacity was really tiny.

I had been given a grant by the Navy Historical Society for another project, so I was able to spend time in Washington, and although the research I did for the grant did not match our quest, I did get back to the Library of Congress for some filler information on the Hump flights. I was also compiling information about Jim, finding out things about him I never knew. Riverside Military Academy sent me a copy of his transcript for his year there and included information about his years at New Trier and Howe Military Academy, which confirmed some of my early recollections of his deeds and misdeeds. I was fortunate to get his complete Air Transport Auxiliary file from the RAF, which included his contract, a record of his number of hours in each aircraft, plus an actual personnel file listing his pretty unruly flying habits, which caused his one-year contract to be terminated after ten months. It made a fairly complete picture of my young cousin, a picture that differed only slightly from my memory. The ATA experience was certainly his pivotal moment since it led to his CNAC hiring and his death in China.

Unfortunately, the Browne family disappeared with Hadda's death in 1957, so there are no photos of him except his graduation photo from Riverside. In all this we did build the image of a young man who loved aviation, lived somewhat on the edge of wild, but was conscious of a world that was headed for perilous times and wanted to be a part of it all.

My retirement from the FDIC in December 1993 gave us both more time, but other projects seemed to get in the way. I was asked to do a banking assignment for two months in Cluj-Napoca, Romania, just before my retirement and found I liked the role and the travel at someone else's expense. That led to assignments in some strange locations, but I enjoyed them all. I taught bank examiners in Petrozavodsk, Russia, on the Finnish border, then traveled to a bank in Warsaw and one in Szczecin, Poland. Later I went to Moldova, and had several projects in the Russian Far East. I got to go on safari in Uganda while working with a bank in Kampala; saw the old gulags in Magadan, Siberia; and even wound up in Baghdad in 2005. All that slowed my CNAC search effort, but with long lapses between my overseas projects I could still stay partly focused on Jim.

Just as our passion for the research had dimmed somewhat, I found the website CNAC.org. Tom Moore, its webmaster, had compiled comprehensive information on the airline. His site had details of the organization, its history, a site for every pilot, mechanic, navigator, and operational staff, and photos from all parts of CNAC's existence.

There was some confusion about our Jim and two other men who spelled their surname "Brown," but Tom and I worked it out, and I learned more than ever about this strange airline that had been so important to China. The website doubled our interest in continuing to piece together what we could on Jim, CNAC, and CNAC No. 60. Tom also convinced us that we needed to get to the reunion in San Francisco. We could not make it that year but did get there in 2004, and it opened more doors.

CNAC reunions became important to us in the next few years. Among the attendees were several of the wartime CNAC pilots, the most celebrated of whom was Moon Fun Chin, a Chinese American who joined CNAC back in 1935 and still was as spry and as sharp as ever. Pete Goutiere was another who shared many a laugh with us, and Dick Rossi, a former Flying Tiger who remembered John Dean from AVG days. The reunion programs were informal but always brought out memories of the pilots themselves or the experiences of the second generation, who carried on the association in grand style.

When we traveled to San Francisco for the reunion, we stayed on to research at the Hoover Institution on War, Revolution and Peace at Stanford. A number of collections there contained tidbits of information—nothing startling but definitely of interest. We researched there for the next several years, always getting teasing bits that left unanswered questions.

When I think back to those early days of our search, I remember how some of the facts we uncovered about CNAC life troubled me. One case that stuck in my mind was that of Jim Scoff. He was an unlikely character whose background is a mystery but who became a CNAC legend, probably for the wrong reasons. In the CNAC *Cannon Ball* issue of May 2004, CNAC pilot Robbie Robertson remembered Scoff: "He was in individual if you ever knew one. God knows how old he was. His home was somewhere in California, and I think he came from the Ferry Command. Jimmy had a chubby round face, curly hair and eyes that rolled in all directions when he was talking. Also, when he got excited, he started to drool and mumble. He would tell the most hair-raising tales after a trip."[1]

Scoff had a love for the ladies and a fondness for alcohol. At one time he shot the lock off a "house of the night" in Calcutta that had closed for the night, which he felt was unfair to potential customers. Stories of some of his episodes are repeated even today at CNAC reunions. Two stand out. First was a landing he made in rainy weather at Dinjan in May 1944. As he landed, his C-47 skidded and slid violently into a parked B-25. The B-25 happened to be the personal airplane of a major general. The general came out and surveyed the wreckage of both planes and asked Scoff, "Do you know who I am?" Scoff stared back at the general with an unlit cigarette dangling from his mouth and his clothes in disarray and said, "No!" "I'm General Old!" After Jim considered that for a minute, he snapped his heels together, saluted smartly, and returned, "And I'm Field Marshall Scoff!" As a civilian Scoff could not be touched even by a general, so he walked away without a reprimand.

On another flight Scoff's plane, given an incorrect heading by the radio tower, wound up lost and running out of gas, so he ordered the crew to bail out and jumped himself. But his chute caught on the door handle and he stayed attached to the doomed plane. With just seconds to spare before hitting the treetops he managed to free himself and opened his chute. His crew was safe, but his reputation as a pilot suffered. His only complaint, according to legend, was that he had had two paychecks in his pocket, uncashed.

But his luck ran out on October 7, 1944, when he was flying CNAC No. 101, a C-47, from Suifu to Dinjan in really bad weather. His flight was reported missing when he failed to arrive. Subsequent investigation indicated that the wings, found hundreds of feet away from the fuselage, had come off in flight and the fuselage had dropped intact, cockpit first, and buried itself in the ground. According to Fletcher Hanks, all that was found of Jim Scoff was a red sweater. But when searchers came on the scene they found the soles of his shoes under the sweater. When they tried to remove the shoes, Scoff's feet were still in them.

The thought of our Jimmie's ending that way bothered me and kept the spark of the search alive when it seemed so fruitless. Two feet sticking out of the ground seemed a poor way to spend eternity, so we pressed on.

Probably the most interesting moment in the 2004 reunion was meeting Clayton Kuhles, president and chief mountaineer of MIA Recoveries, Inc. of Prescott, Arizona, recently returned from a trip through the Himalayas, having discovered three of the twenty-two downed World War II aircraft he eventually found. Clayton and I had several conversations, and he wound up saying, "I can find your cousin's plane." Until that time I had little hope that Jim would be found with the scarcity of information we had turned up. But after Clayton's words, I gave the possibility a lot of thought. That was the point when I began to believe that an actual search could be done.

A couple of years passed, and Donna and I felt drawn closer and closer to the quest. As part of the research we decided to go to China, starting with a visit to Shanghai and Beijing on a river cruise in 2006. In getting ready we found two sites we wanted to visit: the Monument to the Aviator Martyrs in the War of Resistance against Japanese Aggression in Nanjing and the Chennault Flying Tiger Museum in Chungking. So we arranged to leave the ship to make the two side trips.

The ship left from Shanghai, then was to stop in Suchow to see the canal city and its gardens. Instead we planned to meet the ship in Nanjing after taking in the Monument to the Aviator Martyrs. Here's what I wrote describing our first encounter with this truly remarkable testimony to the cost of war:

> In the city of Nanjing, China, on a meticulously manicured hillside, stands a most impressive monument listing the names of Allied Aviators who died or are missing while fighting the Japanese in their war against China from 1931 to 1945. It is no coincidence that the majority of names carved on the thirty-one marble cenotaphs are those of American flyers. Each individual marble stone is engraved with the name and rank of aviators from China, the U.S., Russia and Korea. In English there are 2,186 names of Americans lost in the skies over

China, as well as the names of 870 Chinese flyers, 236 Soviets and 2 Koreans, memorialized in their native language.

Few Americans even know such a memorial exist, and sadly, few Chinese know either. Our visit to the Monument was not part of the tour schedule so we arranged for a guide to take us from the ship to the monument. Even though our Chinese guide was from the area she and the driver had to stop twice to ask directions, the last time just one block from the site.

In some ways it is reminiscent of the Vietnam Wall, with the names of the lost etched deeply into the marble. Over the years erosion of the stones has added drippings down the seams of the stones, almost as if tears were falling among the dead.

Describing the setting of the hillside memorial is difficult; it is beautiful, moving, quiet, and very carefully maintained. From the road there are some 100 steps leading up to a ledge with individual stones for the early fliers, those killed in the Sino-Japanese war, as early as 1932. Then on up about 150 more steps to the plateau on which the memorial rests. Facing the memorial, a section of Chinese names is on the right, Soviets next, then the Americans in the center and on the left.

In front of the black marble cenotaphs is a 50 foot obelisk with the inscription "Monument to the Martyr Aviators in the War of Resistance Against Japan" in English on one side and in Chinese on the other side. Flanking the pillar of stone are statues of two American pilots in their flying togs, pointing skyward, and two Chinese fliers, ready for flight, pointing in the same direction. The whole site is surrounded by pine trees and hardwoods, singing with the wind, whispering through the day and night as if trying to tell the stories of these valiant men of aviation.

It is sad that the surroundings of the site have been neglected, the memorial standing alone as a symbol of order and dignity. Near the Memorial is an area of tenement-like housing, industrial plants, an unpaved, broken road and litter, but the memorial is neat and tidy, thanks to the tender care of its custodian who for thirty-seven years has tended the grounds. If you turn your back on the road and the area behind and concentrate on the arch of welcome, you feel its beauty and its purpose.

In my original description I said there were thirty-one stones, but in reality there are sixty-nine stones bearing the names of the bright young men from America, China, Russia, and Korea that helped protect China and gave their lives in the process.

The monument was begun in 1932, dedicated to the heroes of the air war against Japan who died early in that conflict. Then, as the war expanded, Russia came to China's aid for a while, until they were viciously attacked by Germany. Next the U.S. joined the fight and suffered the greatest losses in the air.

The names on the memorial are the names of bomber pilots and crews, fighter pilots, and transport fliers. Many are transport pilots who lost their lives on the Hump, flying the unglamorous transports in the unglamorous role of aerial truck drivers. They were youngsters and grizzled veterans. Many are buried in sites all over the China-Burma-India theater, and many lie where their aircraft took them, unrecovered in remote parts of the mountains or the seas. To date there are few efforts to recover the lost fliers who occupy the wreckage known as the Aluminum Trail. This memorial is the closest thing many have to a gravesite, far from home, their resting site unknown to most of those in their native country.

The memorial was built with donations from people and organizations all over the world, many from the nations memorialized, but also from other sources. There are big plans for expanding the area to include reflecting ponds and more about the history of aviation in China, but these plans are on hold, waiting for more donations. Given the current state of relations between China and the United States, it may be some time before the expansion comes to pass. I recorded my thoughts after our visit, believing that the Chinese would probably not finish their planned expansion program, and in this I was badly mistaken.

My cousin's name is there, Browne, J. S. c/p 1944–11/17. The year 1944 is wrong; it should have been 1942. But seeing his name among the many others gave me the feeling that he was among friends. Somewhere in the rugged peaks and crevices of the Himalayas, my twenty-one-year-old cousin, his pilot, John J. Dean, and radioman, K. L. Yang, became the first CNAC fliers to die while struggling to deliver the supplies necessary to keep China in the war.

It is some comfort to know that China, despite its turmoil during the past sixty years, still remembers the sacrifices others made for them. These Russians and Americans were aware of the hazards of the life they chose, but were willing to put their lives at risk for an unfamiliar nation and an unfamiliar people. These were airmen as well as patriots, and for the most part they were there because they accepted the challenges of flight in wartime, over unforgiving territory, in antiquated equipment. Even during the last days of the war, flying was at best a very dangerous business.

The existence of this site, however, has brought no improvement in U.S. relations with Chinese leaders, nor have the other Chinese monuments dedicated to the sacrifices of Americans in the fight with Japan. Nowhere in the Chinese government have we found the compassion needed to allow our family to complete the circle of Jim's life. Judging by recent events in China, including the honoring of its Allies in World War II at the seventieth anniversary of the end of its war with Japan, there does seem to be a general recognition of the U.S. role in the war. What the future may bring between our two nations is unknown, but this lovely place immortalizes the dangerous era when our two nations stood side by side, sharing the burdens and risks of war against a common enemy. I have visited the site twice since that first visit and found remarkable changes. Those changes have been made possible by donations from individuals and associations who have provided these funds in recent years. That seems to match the warmth we as individual Americans have felt when mingling with individual Chinese. In our trips in 2006, in 2010, in 2015, and most recently in 2018, we were treated as truly special guests.

# 12

## China National Aviation Corporation Association

The China National Aviation Corporation Association has survived long after most of its original members have left the scene. Their descendants have become the leaders and are determined to keep the organization alive. In our research we have seen many World War II organization websites disappear as their original members dropped away, but the enthusiasm and dedication of this association is unique, and it has been able to gradually fill leadership roles as the originals passed from the scene. The current president is Peggy Maher, who took office when her father, longtime president Bill Maher, died several years ago.

The board is now made up entirely of second-generation CNAC-ers. Peggy's dad was a captain in CNAC at the end of the war; Treasurer Valerie Parish Kendrick's father was Capt. C. C. Parish, who was in charge of the Peking CNAC office right after the war and stayed till the end; he was killed in a plane crash years later. Eve Coulson, who does the newsletter *Cannon Ball*, is the granddaughter of Capt. Bert Coulson, who parachuted successfully from a disabled C-47 and made it back to the field.

As of this writing there are two surviving pilots, both over one hundred years of age, Moon Chin and Pete Goutiere. Moon Chin invites all reunion attendees to his Hillsborough, California, home during the convention for a sumptuous evening meal, always a highlight. Pete, a real entertainer and storyteller, is the author of a book about his experiences in China, *Himalayan Rogue*. Lately he and I have exchanged reminiscences, and I still chuckle at his anecdotes.

Moon Chin's is an amazing story. He was born in 1913 in China, although his father was a U.S. citizen. His family returned to the U.S. when Moon Chin was in school, and he finished high school in Baltimore. At twenty he returned to China, looking for work, and was hired by CNAC in 1935 as a mechanic. He started flying as a copilot soon after and became a captain in 1936. He flew many Hump flights during the war.

Moon Chin's most famous flight was in April 1942, when he picked up a ragged American lieutenant colonel headed to Rangoon. On the way they stopped in Myitkyina, Burma, where Japanese soldiers were closing in on the airport and shoving, shouting, panicked refugees began piling into the aircraft. In a plane that normally held twenty-one passengers, they just kept coming. At one point the colonel asked Moon Chin if he knew what he was doing. Finally, after seventy had boarded, Moon Chin was able to close the door, fight his way to the cockpit, and take off. When they landed in Rangoon, he learned that the colonel was Jimmy Doolittle, on his way home after his carrier-based B-25 raid on Tokyo. Doolittle looked at Moon Chin and said something like, "If I had known what this flight was like, I would have gone home the way I came!"[1]

Moon Chin stayed with CNAC until 1946, when he found higher a paycheck at China's Central Aviation Transport Corporation. He was a leading figure in that airline and in 1951 founded his own airline, Foushing Air, which served cities around Taiwan for years with Moon Chin as its board chairman. He was awarded the Distinguished Flying Cross and the Air Medal for his service in World War II, although he never served in the military. In 2010 he was given a special award for his years of service to aviation in Asia by the Association of Asia Aviation Professionals.

Pete Goutiere also stayed with aviation after his CNAC days. But he is probably best known for his hunting skills and hobnobbing with the aristocrats of India, where he was born and developed a knack for the local language. He emigrated to the U.S.

in 1928, became a U.S. citizen on November 9, 1939, and as the war approached he polished his aviation skills and decided to enlist in the U.S. Army Air Corps. The problem was he was six months over the age limit and the air corps had its pick of men, so he was rejected.

He found a job with Pan Am, delivering P-40s to Cairo, but as soon as he arrived that contract was canceled, so he decided to return to India. In Calcutta he met a CNAC pilot, Cliff Groh, who gave him a pitch for the airline. So he bummed a ride to Chabua, the army base ten miles from Dinjan, got a jeep ride to Dinjan, walked into the office, and immediately got a job.

Goutiere had his share of adventures while flying the Hump and partying with fellow pilots in Calcutta, Chungking, and various cities and villages in between. In his book he described the aircraft he flew:

> All these aircraft, I might add, were mostly Pan Am DC-3s, now converted to freighters, and were called C-53s. For conversion the flooring was replaced with heavy plywood. They could also be used as passenger [planes], but [with] only side rows or bucket seats. They did not have any super-chargers (two-stage blowers) as they were called, for the engines to go to higher altitudes. . . . The planes also lacked proper de-icing equipment or boots, for the leading edge of the wings; propeller deicing was sometimes negligent. For cabin and cockpit heating, we had the old steam heaters. The reservoir was located near the radio operator's chair. It never worked. Once in a while when it did, it usually blew up at high altitudes. Some of the planes had conventional magnetic compasses, located up front above the glare shields, near the instrument panel. A few had the old boat-type compasses, the large one, placed just rear of the pedestal on the floor. Some aircraft did not have artificial horizons, only the old needle-ball system. They had two red warning lights at the instrument panel for the low fuel pressure indicators. Some of the auto-pilots worked, some didn't. Most aircraft had the manual or left-right directional finders for radio navigation. These planes weighed about 2000 pounds less than the C-47s that were to come. The C-47s were constructed for cargo; they had heavy metal flooring, with proper tie-down mechanisms and bucket seats,

all weather operations for deicing and auto-pilots, automatic direction finders and artificial horizons, and paddle-bladed propellers, and two-stage blowers for high altitudes. Ships 60 or better were equipped with a lot of this. 50 series did not have many of these goodies.[2]

Since Jimmie's C-47 was the first one sent under the lend-lease plan, it is doubtful that it had all the refinements Pete listed. Although Fletcher Hanks noted that No. 60 was the first with a blower, records indicate that the first blower on a C-47 did not appear until early 1943. In any event, it can be said that the plane was furnished with only basic instrumentation and communication equipment.

Pete went through a series of aviation jobs after he left CNAC. He wound up flying for Orient Airways, then married for the third time. After that he hired on as a pilot for a maharajah in India, then wound up in Miami in 1952, flying copilot for National Airlines. Next was a stint in the Middle East and then Africa. Ten years later he joined the Federal Aviation Administration, serving in Lebanon, Italy, Jordan, and elsewhere. He married for the fourth and last time and retired. And he regales us with tales of hunting, drinking, flying, and his marriages. At 102 he can still pass for a much younger man.

Several members have written books about CNAC personnel. I finished one in 2008 titled *An Airline at War: The Story of China National Aviation Corporation and Its Men*; Nancy Allison wrote of her father, one of CNAC's principal players in both early and later airline years; and Barry Martin wrote a book on Royal Leonard's aviation years. Barry furnished me with much of the Leonard-Browne correspondence, for which I am most grateful. The most recent book is one published in 2012, *China's Wings*, by Gregory Crouch, the definitive work on the airline's history.

# 13

## MIA Recoveries, Inc.

MIA Recoveries, Inc. is basically a one-man operation. That man, Clayton Kuhles of Prescott, Arizona, has taken on the task of locating downed aircraft from World War II. His efforts had been largely self-funded until the latest financial slump, requiring the last mission to be partly funded by donations. Clayton has been a mountaineer for many years, concentrating in the Burma area and parts of northeastern India. Most of his discoveries have been in India's Arunachal Pradesh Province, unfortunately now the site of an India-China territorial dispute which jeopardized several missions conducted by the Joint POW/MIA Accounting Command (JPAC), a task force of the U.S. Department of Defense until it was deactivated in 2015.

Clayton was a very successful businessman in Prescott, but he craved more excitement than his day-to-day business provided, so he took to the mountains and climbed some very impressive heights before turning his skills to the finding of aircraft. Besides being chronicled on the MIA Recoveries website, many of his finds are documented in a massive work of aircraft crashes in the China-Burma-India theater, *The Aluminum Trail* by Chick Marrs Quinn.

*The Aluminum Trail*, written by the widow of a Hump crash pilot, is one of the most compelling volumes of the World War II air war. Although it is limited to the China-Burma-India theater, it is amazingly accurate and details the cost of our air support in that theater. Briefly, it documents 696 fatal crashes in which 3,498 passengers and crew lost their lives and 1,022 were declared dead but originally classified as missing. That includes not only Hump crashes but those of combat aircraft all the way from L-5 spotter aircraft to B-29s, with their ten- or eleven-men crews. Figures published by the U.S. Air Force indicate that 594 aircraft were lost on the Hump, killing 1,314 passengers and crew, plus 81 planes never accounted for with their 345 crew members (among them, Jim Browne). *The Aluminum Trail* documents 375 Hump crashes but recognizes that because planes were lost so rapidly, those crashes often were never recorded.[1]

All these facts presented Clayton with a remarkable potential for sighting, since almost none of these planes was recovered. They lay where they fell, although scavengers sometimes cut up the aircraft and made use of the metal to fashion primitive pots and pans. But for scavengers to be interested, planes had to be reasonably accessible at the lower altitudes. Sometimes aircraft in trouble would jettison their cargo to lose weight, trying to maintain altitude, and that would draw the locals to the site.

In its early days CNAC would fly banknotes into China from India to supply currency for the public. In several cases planes got into trouble over the mountains and had to jettison the currency. Joey Thom was a young Chicago-born Chinese pilot flying currency when he ran into a fierce thunderstorm he could not avoid without hitting mountains on either side of him. He told his crew to dump the currency, which they did, but it was too late. His plane smacked into the side of a mountain near Guilin and he and his crew perished. Soon afterward, the citizens of Guilin showed signs of new wealth; the authorities reported the economic boom, which drew attention to Thom's flight path, and the wreckage was soon spotted by Moon Chin. In CNAC No. 60's case villagers reported that tin was discovered on river banks near the crash site, a clue to its flight path.

Clayton's first discovery occurred in October 2003, when he found the wreckage of a C-87 (the cargo version of a B-24). Records indicate it originated in Yangkai, China, on April 24, 1943, and was headed across the Hump to the U.S. Army base at Chabua, India.

It crashed at 13,200 feet in Arunachal Pradesh Province in India, killing its crew of five. MIA Recoveries salvaged a few human remains and turned them over to the U.S. Consulate, which transferred them to JPAC. One crew member—Pfc Mervyn E. Sims, twenty-three, from Healdsburg, California—was identified and his remains sent home. It was Clayton, not JPAC, who was responsible for that success.

Located nearby was the wreckage of a C-47, CNAC No. 77, which was flown by Russell Coldren with three Chinese crew members who died with him on January 6, 1945. Their flight from Kunming was originally scheduled to land at Tengchong, China, but weather in China was closing in on the flight paths, so Coldren opted to change his destination to the home base at Dinjan. The deviation did nothing to change the fate of the aircraft; the wreckage was found in Burma on a mountain.

Clayton's next find was the following month, November 2003, when he found another C-47 with its three-man crew. The plane took off from Yunnan Yi and was supposed to land at an air corps base in Misamari, India, but never made it there. The date was November 2, 1943; the weather was good and there was no radio transmission after take-off. In October of the following year a search team spotted the wreckage and sent a ground team to the site. They were able to identify the crew and buried them there.

Next, in December 2005, Clayton found another CNAC C-53. This one was even higher than the others, at fifteen thousand feet. Pilot Joe Rosbert and Ridge Hammill with Chinese radioman Y. T. Wong had been trying to get over the mountains from Dinjan to Kunming, but heavy ice forced them to lower altitudes, so they opted to return to Dinjan but grazed a mountaintop and slid to a stop on a ridge just below the peak. The radioman was killed on impact, but pilot and copilot, both injured, walked for an agonizing forty-seven days before they reached the army field at Sadiya, India. Rosbert survived the war, but Hammill was killed in a CNAC crash in 1945.

Just a year later, in December 2006, Clayton discovered a B-24 that had left Kunming on January 25, 1944, with a Chabua destination, flying in a formation of other B-24s. The weather closed in; the plane lost the formation and found a ten-thousand-foot mountain while flying at nine thousand feet. The wreck contained the bodies of all eight crew members and again is located in Arunachal Pradesh.

On Clayton's next trip, in October 2007, he found a C-46 that had left Kunming on February 20, 1944, destined for India's base at Misamari. With bad weather closing in, the pilot appeared to be lost. There was radio confusion as bearings came from two bases. The pilot wanted to bail out but was talked out of it. Wreckage was found at eight thousand feet with the crew of four listed as missing. This was also in Arunachal Pradesh.

Also in October 2007 Clayton found a C-109 with a crew of four, all killed in the crash. It was, again, in Arunachal Pradesh, this time at 8,200 feet. Four had been killed in the next wreckage he found, that of a C-46 out of Chabua at only 4,000 feet. Weather was the culprit once again, and the end came in Arunachal Pradesh with the others. Next was a B-24 with a crew of ten, heading for assignment with the 308th Bombardment Group in Kunming but crashing at only 2,900 feet, cause unknown. It was located in September 2008.

One of the worst was a C-46 carrying two pilots and thirty-three passengers headed for Karachi, India, and then home. This one developed engine trouble, caught fire, and slammed into a mountain. One man, Tech Sergeant Marvin H. Jacobs, survived, thanks to a local hunter who sheltered him, then organized a workforce to hack out a rough landing strip so a small plane could take him out. Clayton found that wreckage in September 2008.

The MIA Recoveries list goes on. A C-47 with four aboard on a July 13, 1943, flight was discovered in September 2008. It crashed in Arunachal Pradesh at 6,400 feet, trying to get from India to Kunming. In October 2008 Clayton found a C-46 that left Changyi, China. Even though winds of eighty to one hundred miles per hour were reported at altitude plus severe icing, the plane kept to its schedule. After take-off, nothing was heard from the plane. Clayton discovered that its four-man crew had died on impact. Also in the fall of 2008 Clayton found a C-87, about which there was little information. It left China and was due to arrive in Jorhat, India, but, like so many others, it never arrived. Five died in the unforgiving mountains when the aircraft was lost. A C-87 from Chabua went down on its way to China, carrying six to their deaths. No cause for the crash was reported; "it simply disappeared while en route over the Hump." The wreckage was found by Clayton and local guides on October 16, 2008, at nine thousand feet in Arunachal Pradesh. A C-47 on a May 17, 1946, flight carried a crew of three plus a Graves Registration team of six and two other passengers. It also had on board the remains of forty-two POWs who had died in Rangoon prison camps. It was found in November 2009. Four planes were found on one of the longest expeditions, from November 2010 to January 2011. Two were C-47s, one with a crew of three, and the other with seven aboard. One was found in Bhutan at thirteen thousand feet, the other in Arunachal Pradesh, also at thirteen thousand feet. The other two were B-24s from the 308th Bomb Group; both had left China for Chabua but never arrived. The first flight was on January 25, 1944, the other on May 25, 1944.

These aircraft, plus the three Clayton found on his last trip in his search for Jim's CNAC No. 60, are representative of the number of aircrews that still lie where they died, despite our government's knowledge of their location. Granted, there are many obstacles to overcome to actually recover and identify a set of remains, but the initial step of investigating the crash sites must be taken. Without that effort, no remains can be brought home.

Both India and China were our Allies in World War II, yet we do not seem able to convince them that recovery efforts in their territory are the right thing to do. If we cannot convince these nations of that fact, how do we expect to solve the really difficult problems between countries?

While many nations do not go to the extremes the U.S. does to bring home their dead, Japan is an exception. Every year a delegation comes to Saipan to scour the little island for bones of Japanese soldiers who died there. The island is riddled with caves that, in many cases, were simply sealed by blasting their entrances. These caves were excavated every year and remains were recovered. On the beaches at the end of the search, the bones would be cremated, the ashes boxed and brought back to Japan, then distributed to relatives of the dead soldiers.

One fact bothered Clayton: after he notified JPAC of his finds, he would compile a list of airmen on each airplane, yet none of the U.S. Army agencies notified families that their loved ones had been found. He was told that the discovery could not be formally substantiated except by JPAC, and they were reluctant to notify families without their searching the wreck site themselves. So the families of the 193 crewmen have never been told by our government that their missing aircraft have been found. Clayton found this practice to be cruel to the families, not allowing them some peace that their relative had been found.

He searched through army records for the last known manifest of crew and passengers of the downed planes he had discovered. In later stages of the war units were required to issue a Missing Aircrew Report citing the details of the mission and the names of the crew and passengers. Still it was not always possible to find relatives of crew members, but he and others made every effort to notify the affected families, possibly creating some hard feelings with JPAC or other military personnel.

By 2010 the financial downturn had caught up with Clayton's enterprises in Prescott. Up until that time, a few donations to MIA Recoveries had trickled in over the years, but the bulk of his costs he paid out of his own pocket. His expenses on most journeys were kept to a minimum. He traveled alone, prepping for each trip as best he could, then finding locals with knowledge of either the mountainous areas or the history of air tragedies in their regions. He organized the search crews from those living near the wreck site, providing them with food and necessities purchased from local sources. His average expenses amounted to roughly $ $30,000 to $50,000, depending mostly on the length of his stay. But after 2010 funds were hard to come by, and 2011 was to be his last trip unless things changed.

After a critical analysis by Congress, JPAC was merged with the Defense POW/Missing Personnel Office to form the Defense POW/MIA Accounting Agency (DPAA), which announced that it was going to try to privatize some of its activities. MIA Recoveries has contacted DPAA several times, requesting information on the bid process for China-Burma-India expeditions. Clayton was told that a preliminary search by JPAC would run roughly $500,000 to $1,000,000, in contrast to his $30,000 to $50,000, so privatizing would make the government funds go much further and allow more searches. Also, he was able to get into crash sites in a low-key operation, whereas JPAC had required high-level diplomatic and political involvement. Presently, politics in China, Burma, and India are preventing excavations in the area. And he has not even received a response to his repeated proposals to DPAA. Our government could at least listen to his proposal.

Clayton's last trip to the China-Burma-India theater was in the fall of 2011. That was "our" trip, the search for CNAC No. 60, but Clayton had broadened his goals to look for several other sites in northeastern India. He had been close to finding several wrecks in previous trips, so he vowed to make full use of this adventure.

He knew exactly where he wanted to search for Jim's plane, but when he arrived in China in September 2011, the weather was intimidating. In spite of two tries, he was unable to reach the area. He decided to wait for a break in the weather on Cangshan Mountain, but when bad weather continued, he went back to India to see if he could locate ships he had missed on his previous India missions. He left Dali on October 7 with the hope of making another ascent before going back to the U.S.

On his side trip to India he found a C-46 that apparently had been flying in bad weather with winds at seventy miles per hour. The report in *The Aluminum Trail* indicated a sudden event had occurred, so sudden there was no Mayday call from the pilot. Clayton found the wreckage in Arunachal Pradesh at twelve thousand feet on the ancestral hunting grounds of the Towsit family. A family member took him to the site, telling Clayton that his father had first visited the location in 1962. Four died in the crash.

The second find was a B-25 that was piloted by John L. "Blackie" Porter. Porter was on a rescue mission in his B-25 when he was shot down by a Japanese Zero. Porter managed to push his copilot, 2nd Lt. James Spain, out the top hatch, and Spain parachuted to safety, but all five others on board died at the scene. No remains were found, but Clayton did find the dog tags of Sgt. Harry D. Tucker, gunner.

That loss on December 10, 1943, was a real blow to the search-and-rescue efforts of the U.S. Army Air Corps, and it took some time to recover. Blackie Porter was a charismatic leader in the search-and-rescue cause, having created the first squadron formed for the exclusive use of searching for lost aircraft. In later years medics and specialists would parachute into the forbidding jungle to aid the injured and lead the survivors out to safety.

After reporting these two locations to JPAC, Clayton returned to China to try again to find Jim.

# 14

## China Beckons

It was at the 2009 CNAC convention in San Francisco that CNAC board member Eve Coulson and I began to talk about a trip to China. A number of years before, the association had organized a China tour, and Eve and I felt that it was time to go back. Donna and I talked to several other members during our four days in San Francisco and found a number who asked to be included if a trip were to be planned.

Donna had been the manager of a travel agency in Florida in previous years, so we decided to check into possible itineraries, costs, timing, and the many details that would be required. We also had a real advantage in Diego Kusak, son of Steve Kusak, a CNAC pilot during the war years. Diego lived in Kunming and had been promoting CNAC in local venues ever since he moved there several years earlier. He not only offered to help in the planning but offered a number of suggestions on places to visit and where we might get some free hotel stays.

So in the fall of 2009 we started our preparations. We polled the association members and found twenty who tentatively committed to make the trip, which gave us enough confidence to start the real planning. First, we wanted to make the trip meaningful to the CNAC membership, so we deviated from the usual route and focused on Yunnan Province, where Kunming, with so much CNAC history, was located.

In early 2010 we perfected our plan and had seventeen signed up with departure in October of that year. Our itinerary began in Hong Kong, then on to Kunming, Lushui, Pianma, Dali, and home from Shanghai. It was a wonderful time for us, and we got to see much of the country where some of our relatives spent the war years. The bus ride from Lushui to Pianma really gave us a feeling for the rugged Himalayas, even though the route passed only through the foothills.

We opted to fly into Hong Kong and spend a few days before heading for Kunming, where Diego found a hotel that would host us for several days. He also persuaded a number of eateries who were interested enough in our CNAC history to feed us—no charge.

Hong Kong had changed drastically since our last visit, but one landmark that looked familiar was the old Peninsula Hotel in Kowloon. We were invited to go to the top of the hotel, where we could stand on the heliport and look out at the new structures visible in all directions. It was magnificent! The visit was a real treat, thanks to Peter DeKantzow, son of a CNAC pilot, who lives in Hong Kong.

After the short flight to Kunming, we found Diego and our hotel, where we were treated like royalty. In our group was probably the main reason we were treated so well, the CNAC pilot Moon Fun Chin, already famous in China. He had joined CNAC in 1935 as a mechanic and was one of the first Chinese pilots to make captain. At the time of our visit he was ninety-six years old and was by far the biggest draw of the group.

In Kunming the Hump Monument was the site of a short ceremony that was televised. We were also taken to the end of the Kunming airport runway. There we could see the airport, updated, but still the original CNAC terminus for Hump flights. And here I met Liu Xiatong, a young Chinese author whose book *Flying the Hump* provided clues that were helpful in our search for Jimmie. In one of his chapters we found the words, in English, "James S. Browne and John J. Dean." The translation of those startling words spoke of the last two radio transmissions of CNAC No. 60. They were found in one of China's old radio transmission stations used to guide Hump flights. The transmissions had never been unearthed until Liu discovered the many records of wartime flights. The first transmission was routine, simply saying that they were approaching the hills of the Himalayan range and proceeding normally. Then, just minutes later, came a frantic message saying that they had encountered severe turbulence and were dumping the cargo of tin ingots. Then silence.

Those two messages were critical as Clayton assembled his information for a search. Standing on the threshold of the airport runway, it was impossible not to think of the last, fatal flight of CNAC No. 60 and the final moments of Jimmie's life. Many others in the group had similar thoughts of crew members of CNAC flights that began or ended right here. Tom Moore, the webmaster of CNAC. org, thought of the crash here that killed his uncle, Emil Scott, in March 1942. And Moon Chin thought of his many take-offs and landings in those feverish wartime days. There were many emotions as the sleek new jets thundered overhead in their landing patterns.

On another day we were invited to a special gathering of Yunnan Province officials to honor our group, particularly Moon Chin. Diego had organized the impressive session. In Kunming we were also honored with testimonials for the AVG, the Flying Tigers, whose protection of the city in December 1941 is still remembered with reverence. It was pointed out on several occasions that without the gas and ammunition supplied by CNAC transports, the AVG P-40s would never have left the ground.

Then we moved on to Lushui on the Burma border, where they wined, dined, and entertained us for two nights and provided us with a vintage bus to take us over the foothills of the Himalayas on a truly exciting trip to Pianma. In this tiny village smack on the Burma-China border was one of the highlights of the trip: the restored C-53 of Jim Fox, who was killed trying to get through a mountain pass and crashed in April 1943, only a few months after Jimmie's death. Villagers had carefully and skillfully brought the wreckage, piece by piece, down the mountain and reassembled it with care in a simple museum in Pianma. It was not a perfect restoration—it was missing its right wing—but it was without a doubt a C-53. (As reported earlier, we learned later that the right wing is a featured display at the Kunming Walmart.)

Then it was back on the same tortuous route we had conquered earlier to a grand banquet in our Lushui hotel. That evening we were treated to a ceremonial toast that involved tipping way back in your chair and having a local moonshine poured into your almost upside-down mouth, to the delight of the others. In both Lushui and Pianma, Moon Chin was the focal point of the various ceremonies.

From Lushui we were bused to Dali so we could visit Yunnan Yi, a small village that hosted another of the many radio beacons that steered the Hump pilots through the perilous mountain peaks. We saw the memorial to the Stone-Rollers, where the stones used to flatten airfield runway surfaces still sat by the abandoned airstrip. These huge stones were harnessed to hundreds of Chinese workers and pulled repeatedly over small stones, smashed by hand, to form the hundreds of runways used by Allied planes during World War II.

So many of the Chinese contributions to the air war in the China-Burma-India theater were massive efforts made by uncomplaining peasants who abandoned their fields and their rice paddles to provide the manpower so sorely needed. The huge stones still sitting by an abandoned airstrip were in no small measure a monument to the Chinese who, by sheer numbers, made them modern tools.

Our last stop was Shanghai, where some of us took a day-long trip to Nanjing on the bullet train to see the war memorial and brand-new aviation museum sponsored by the Nanjing Aviation Association. The bullet train itself was a new experience for many; the train's speed was displayed on a speedometer mounted in the front of each car. Scenery sped by to almost dizzying effect. To top it off, it was a national holiday, and the train station was packed. It was really unnerving for our little lady chaperone to try to keep track of the ten of us as we were herded through the train station.

Included in our Nanjing side trip was a typical Chinese luncheon provided by the Nanjing Aviation Association in the park where Sun Yat-sen is buried. He rests in a mausoleum on top of a hill with about 350 steps leading up to it. Only two of the group made it to the top but said it was worth the climb. The restaurant and statues, mausoleum, and beautiful park make up a huge recreational area.

By that time I was getting nervous; we had a train back to Shanghai that we needed to catch, and the visit to Sun Yat-sen's resting place was not part of the itinerary. The main purpose of our side trip was to see the Monument to the Aviator Martyrs in the War of Resistance against Japanese Aggression, plus we had a museum to see following the monument, and time was fleeting.

Our visit to the monument was as moving as it had been in 2006. Fortunately it was a beautiful day and the meticulousness of the maintenance was clearly evident. I think our group was a little startled at the scope of the monument, the names in black marble, the airmen pointing skyward, and the tall obelisk also pointing to the sky. Since the monument sits on the side of a hill, the trees in full blossom form a sort of frame for the large pieces of stone; from the street, the effect is awesome. The second visit was just as stirring as we remembered it, and we were happy to see it once again.

On one of the tablets, Jimmie's name appears twice, both incorrectly. First, he is listed as C/P James S. Brown 11/17/1942, with his name spelled wrong, and next he is identified as C/P James S. Browne 11/17/1944, with the wrong date. On this visit I noticed that John Dean too appeared twice, once as Captain John J. Dean 1942/11/17 and just below it, Dean J J Pilot 1942/11/17.

When we did get to the museum, Donna and I got a big surprise. The new museum, recently opened, housed a number of AVG, CNAC, and Russian artifacts from the war in a wonderfully visitor-friendly setting. But the shocker was that the museum was adjacent to the Martyrs Monument joined by a gentle hillside set of stairs leading to the monument. When we had visited in 2006, there had been a model of the museum-to-come, but no evidence of its feasibility. It looked to us at the time that the monument itself was probably the extent to which the Chinese would honor its deceased Allied airmen. But we were very much mistaken as we toured the moving surroundings of the museum. There were sculptures of deceased pilots, full-size models of vintage aircraft, all in a park-like hillside setting. Inside the museum a speaker played martial Russian music that seemed out of place in the serenity of the whole complex. (After we were back in Florida,

I sent several CDs of Glenn Miller to improve the musical experience.) There were several mockups, including a sandbagged dugout with periodic light and bomb simulations. Many of the articles displayed were Russian as well as American, reminding us of the important part Russia played in early China aviation. In all, I have to say that it is as impressive a museum as we have visited, and we have visited many. With the addition of the museum to the monument acreage, the whole memorial dramatized the respect paid by the Chinese to those who helped them survive the war. While the governments of our two nations might spar and disagree, the monument offers another view of Chinese-American relations.

The setting of the park had changed drastically, too. The empty factories and virtual slums we remembered from our 2006 visit were gone, replaced by handsome new office and apartment buildings. Even the potholed road that led to the site on our first visit was now smooth blacktop. The whole scene was so well done that it gave the impression that the Chinese people and government really did care about those who died for their country.

We finally were herded into our bus and whizzed to the station just in time to join the throngs of holiday crowds, and then zipped back to Shanghai on the bullet train. It was a wonderful day.

That night we had been asked to include a presentation of some kind, but it was very vague, and we had had a long day, so I had been reluctant to include it. But it was to honor Moon Chin, so it was scheduled. It turned out to be a very impressive gathering of officials and other guests representing the Association of Asia Aviation Professionals from Singapore to honor three men who had contributed so much to aviation in the Orient with the Distinguished Asian Aerospace Professional Award. Moon Chin was one of the three, and his aviation credentials were listed and discussed. It was probably the most impressive record of accomplishment of any previous honoree, including the other two recipients, both deceased. The total history of aviation in the Orient was represented by these three honorees. It was further testimony to the many years of service Moon Chin had given and the respect he had earned from both his peers and the aviation public.

Our last event in Shanghai was a meeting with our former translator, Joy, a young Chinese woman whom we had met in Shanghai in 2003, when Donna and I were both teaching English to Chinese bankers and teaching them about lending practices in America. Joy had been a delightful companion; we kept up a correspondence with her and saw her again when we took a Yangtze River cruise in 2006. Our time with her was short because of our schedules, but we did manage to have a KFC Fried Chicken dinner in our hotel room with much catch-up conversation.

That was our final event on our Chinese trip, and I thought back to our meeting in Kunming with author Liu Xiatong, who had brought to light the last two transmissions of CNAC No. 60. We didn't know then that when we were in Dali we were only a few kilometers from the crash site we had been looking for all those years.

# 15

## Planning Begins

The first time we met, at a CNAC reunion, Clayton had promised to find Jimmie's plane. Neither of us had much to go on aside from the plane's point of departure. We learned that the weather had not been the best and that there had been little Japanese air activity, but weather over the Hump defied forecasting and even reporting. Still, Clayton had some contacts in China who offered insights into activity there during the war.

In November 1942 few aircraft of any kind flew over the villages of Yunnan Province, and numbers of locals now remembered the air crashes very vividly. In all the records we had examined, the book *We Flew without Guns* contained one of the only references to Jim's fatal flight other than this entry in *The Aluminum Trail*: "This flight left Kunming for Dinjan and was overdue. It is now presumed missing."[1] We also knew of the entry in the minutes of the CNAC Board of Directors meeting in 1943, a brief mention of the two fatal crashes in 1942, Jim's and Emil Scott's March 1942 crash at Kunming.

Those sketchy references were the only clues we had to go on, but Clayton began to draw some hypothetical routes that Jim may have taken. At the same time he made other trips to the area, although not to China, but picked up information from various sources. He found a former U.S. Army L-5 pilot, Arthur Clark, who had flown over the lower Himalayas during the war and remembered seeing the wreckage of a C-47 in the Dali area. Clark also made inquiries of locals who lived in the area who remembered their parents talking about a downed plane high up in the Cangshan Mountains. It was all very vague, but it seemed to match the possible routes that Clayton had plotted.

With the new information from China and some verification from Clayton's sources, we decided to begin planning a search for 2011. While we were doing what we could in researching written records filed in so many places, Clayton was doing what he does for all his expeditions. He located a trekker guide and talked him into visiting local villagers, finding those who knew about an aircraft crash in 1942 and asking them if they knew of others who might have knowledge. In the years before our expedition had actually been planned, he had developed a core of people who lived near the crash and had personal exposure to its location. Plus, he had Arthur Clark, the L-5 pilot who had spotted the plane and was ready to assist if he could. He also had Diego Kusak, son of a former CNAC pilot, who was still living in Kunming. He agreed to work with Clayton and scout the Dali area for possible lodgings and contacts.

Clayton also approached the plane from a negative aspect. He analyzed all 696 wrecks listed in *The Aluminum Trail*, which shows most locations for downed aircraft, and found no wrecks reported on Cangshan. In November 1942 that was not surprising since only a few pilots were actually flying the Hump at that time. He figured that the lack of a reported crash site in that book must mean that the wreckage spotted by Clark and the local stories must have been of an early wartime crash, potentially CNAC No. 60. *Aluminum Trail* information was sketchy about flights that took place before 1943. Jim's plane is the second entry in the book but gives no information besides the names of the crew, the plane number, and the date, with vague information about the route taken.

These factors reinforced Clayton's plotting. Meanwhile he was making nearly annual treks through the mountains, mostly in northeastern India and Burma. He was highly successful at finding missing aircraft, but in every case he came on the planes while exploring, not necessarily looking for them. When he arrived in a given area he would talk to the villagers, who were eager to share their knowledge. In November 1942 an aircraft was still a rare sight anywhere over the Hump. By the end of the war, when the reconstruction period began, aircraft of many kinds were daily sights for villagers and hill people alike, and villagers had visited the wreckage several times.

The difference in the search for CNAC No. 60 was that Clayton would need to know precisely where this specific plane would be and head directly there. So he would need more knowledge of his target than in any previous search. Also, he was being funded at least partly by sources other than himself, so he had to be accountable. By 2011 he had picked Clark's brains enough to feel that the wreckage he had spotted and that the villagers remembered was CNAC No. 60.

Unlike in later years, when hundreds of airplanes flew over these villages, in November 1942 only a handful of transports crossed the Hump. At that time it was still very much in doubt as to whether these risky routes could supply the entire Chinese Army as well as fuel the planes planned to be sent to the China-Burma-India theater. That theater was destined to have airpower but few ground troops.

In 2010 I brought back the Chinese version of CNAC 60's last moments, as found in Liu Xiatong's book, which stated that all was well until moments before the crash. That put into question the Genovese report of an in-flight transmission indicating heavy ice earlier in the flight. The two transmissions cited in the Chinese book made a possible new flight path.

Clayton studied the flight characteristics of the C-47, its speed at different stages of flight, its strengths and weaknesses that might affect the path of the aircraft. Weather patterns for the area were not readily available, but weather conditions in general were studied, anything that might give a clue. It should be remembered that many of the older CNAC pilots were from commercial flying, experienced in multi-engine aircraft, but John Dean hailed from navy and AVG training, all in single-engine planes, and Jim was reasonably inexperienced with multi-engine aircraft, although he had flown ferry flights for ATA in two-engine bombers. Both had been with CNAC for only a short time, Dean since August and Jim a few weeks. With their limited experience, the crew might have been unable to handle the blast of turbulent weather over mountainous terrain.

With the knowledge Clayton had accumulated and his own experience, he determined that CNAC No. 60 was the wreckage Clark had seen, and a search, if it could be organized, would center on the peaks of Cangshan. With what he had gleaned from research, from his own trips, from deductions, from Liu, and on just his own intuition, we decided to seek funds for a search in 2011. It still is amazing to me how he became so convinced that the exact location he predicted would yield the long-lost wreckage, but it obviously was the key to success.

# 16

## The Frustration of Fund-raising

As the wheels of progress moved slowly forward and our facts kept mounting, by the end of 2010, after we came back from China, Clayton and I had committed to a search. We were working different sides of the street; Donna and I were concentrating on Liu Xiatong's passages, trying to get as specific as we could with the numerous translations we had requested, while Clayton was communicating with some leads from Hump days, pilots who recalled wreckage spotted from the air. It was surprising that even after more than seventy years the pilots could bring such detailed information to the search. Both Arthur Clark and Pete Goutiere were sure of the location of the wreckage spotted in the mid-1940s, strengthening our chances of pinpointing the area.

But we knew the next step was to look for funding, and we were optimistic. We were novices at the game but saw so many MIA flags flying, saw so many references to MIAs that we felt a small campaign should do it.

We contacted Gary Zaetz, a Facebook friend, who was extremely active in trying to get JPAC to the scene of his uncle Irving Zaetz's B-24, the *Hot as Hell*, lost in the Assam Valley on January 25, 1944. Gary was a great help, giving us the mailing list he used to promote his own quest. He and his family have devoted their efforts for years to get the lieutenant home. We met Gary's father at our first briefing with the Defense POW/Missing Personnel Office many years ago and learned the frustrating history of their efforts, so similar to ours.

JPAC did a one-time mission to the *Hot as Hell* a number of years ago, but the bomber lies in Arunachal Pradesh in India, as tragic in its crash location as it was in its loss. The Chinese and Indian governments are in a stalemate on borders in that area, and the Indian government has prevented any large search efforts there.

Gary helped us by promoting our cause as well as his own, so we began our fund-raising effort with his group. We were rather unsuccessful, however, primarily because they preferred to donate to their own cause, in retrospect a very logical decision. At that point we discovered an unsurprising fact: most Americans are simply not interested in the MIA problem. It hits very few families on a personal basis, and even most of those feel it is too challenging to tackle on their own. Most reason that only the government has the tools and the organization to deal with the issue. Many organizations pledge to fly the POW/MIA flag as their commitment to the issue, but that ends their involvement. That, coupled with the deluge of requests for money that come to every American on a daily basis, put our drive in jeopardy from the beginning. Not being professionals in the art, we should have known that truth just from the morning's mail. But since it was so important to us, we were confident that others would respond. We had tentatively set a goal of $15,000, which was what Clayton estimated as the costs for a search in China.

Then we turned our attention to our own group, China National Aviation Corporation Association, the ones who knew best about our search. In past years, Fletcher Hanks, a CNAC Hump pilot and active CNAC Association member, had been devoting much of his time and efforts to get to the site of another CNAC crash site. This was pilot Jim Fox's DC-3, which had hit a mountain on the China-Burma border in March 1943. In 1944 Hanks and two others offered to try to find the plane. That effort had to stop short of the wreck when one of the three began to suffer from the altitude and terrain and finally collapsed. It was many years later when Hanks tried again, this time with Chinese Red Army soldiers as his guides. It was 1997, and Hanks was close to eighty years old but still trying to get to Fox's CNAC No. 53. On this ascent he was successful and looked down at the wreckage, awed that he had finally reached his goal.

Some months before, Hanks had organized a fund drive to allow him to make the trip. He drew $30,000 from his friends, fellow pilots, and those who knew about his goal. According to financial data, he used about $15,000 on his trip, which left about $15,000 in the bank. I wrote to him and asked if he would consider letting us use part of that money for our search. His answer was an emphatic no; he intended to use that money himself.

He did make another effort to get back to China, but I believe he fell in a Canadian airport and had to come home. Hanks was a storied character in the annals of CNAC, having married the widow of John Petach of the AVG, who died in its last weeks. Hanks passed away several years ago, and I believe his fund remains in the CNAC bank account.

Next we tried direct mail to veterans' organizations, most of whom had in their mission statement that they encouraged more activity in the search for MIAS, so we were optimistic that one or more might find our project worthwhile. In researching the material for my book on the American intervention into Russia in 1918, I found that when the Americans departed in 1919, they brought home most of the bodies of the expedition members who died in Russia. However, they left behind more than one hundred bodies in Bolshevik territory. Ten years later, in 1929, the Veterans of Foreign Wars organized a return to northern Russia to search for graves; successful, they brought home an additional eighty-six remains. Given that history, we thought the VFW would be the first group to approach. Instead, claiming that being part of such a mission would not be feasible, would be too expensive, and so forth, they were the first to reject our appeal, as would many others in the following days.

Next was the American Legion, which was even briefer in their refusal, citing precedence, other commitments, and the existence of JPAC. We tried Amvets, the Order of the Purple Heart, Disabled American Veterans, and some I don't remember. All of them had mission statements that showed a concern for JPAC and its results, and all of them turned us down. Looking back at the stack of donation requests we get daily, it is hard to say that I did not understand why.

Finally realizing we would get no help from veterans' organizations, we tried to think of more innovative approaches. We did a direct-mail effort sent to CNAC members, family, and friends, Pan American World Airways Historical Foundation members, and any other groups that had what we felt was potential. The results were not encouraging.

In a huge morale booster, we heard from the folks at CNAC Association that they would contribute $5,000 to the cause. Our own family was the next biggest contributor, and the total finally looked almost respectable. We still kept trying, though. We tried celebrities. The comedian Kelsey Grammer was known to be supportive of MIAs and critical of JPAC, so we fired off several gripping messages to him, but got no response. We thought we could cash in on a Vietnam & All Veterans weekend rally to be held in Wickham Park in Melbourne, Florida. We knew Ross Perot would be addressing the vets, so we bought a nice banner, got hold of a canopy and some map boards we made from Clayton's materials, and sat for three days with much conversation but no cash. We netted a minus $67 and never got a glimpse of Perot. Even so, Clayton felt that there would be enough money for a search, and he began to focus on his China contacts and reinforcing what he already knew, gaining a few new facts.

Later, after the search had taken place, we tried another fundraiser, using Indiegogo. We developed a very moving video with testimonials, vintage films, stills, and recordings. It was a lot of fun and did get some results, about $5,000, as I recall. I hope that made up for any out-of-pocket money Clayton spent.

Our experience indicated that fund-raising is more than simply having a worthy project; it takes some real marketing skills. I have kept up a little with Indiegogo and have marveled at the large amounts of money being given for what seem to be really silly projects with no benefit to the world. Some very worthy projects have made out very well, but our effort looked pretty puny in the large scheme of things. Looking back, I think we should have taken a simpler approach; we had too much "stuff" on our site. We made a great effort, but our results have to be judged as at least semi-failures.

# 17

## The Ascent

As Clayton Kuhles and MIA Recoveries, Inc. set out on the search, the mission was simple and straightforward:

1. To verify the accuracy of the location of the search area and locate the best route to get there.

2. To assemble a capable team to make the ascent to the search area and ascend as many times as needed.

3. To locate the airplane, or parts that would establish the make and model of the airplane that crashed, and to obtain from the wreckage an identification number that would positively identify CNAC No. 60 by either the construction number or Douglas Aircraft identification number.

There were, however, preliminaries to allow for the greatest chance for success:

1. To investigate the various sources that had provided information valuable to the coming search. Specifically, to interview Arthur Clark and determine the villages that might have the most pertinent information.

2. To interview as many sources as possible, including second- and third-generation locals who had heard tales of the crash.

With the advice of those most knowledgeable about both the

crash and the topography, Clayton sought the best access to the site. When that was determined, he would hire local young men capable of the rigors of the climb, trying to include at least one climber with knowledge of the crash and its location. Next was to assemble the team and determine the needs of each climber, including footwear, outer clothing, headgear, and rations. Finally, he had to lead the team to the site and, once there, evaluate conditions and visible evidence of the CNAC No. 60, construction number 4618, serial number 41-18556.

In 2011 the CNAC reunion was held in San Francisco on September 7 through 10, and Clayton stopped by on his way to China. During the four-day meeting, he and Liu Xiatong spent time together studying Clayton's search area and reinforcing the strength of his logic. It must have been interesting since Liu spoke no English and Clayton no Chinese. But Clayton reported that the Chinese author was in agreement that the Cangshan area (formerly known as Dali Mountain) was the place on which to focus. To add even more certainty, CNAC wartime pilot Pete Goutiere had several times spotted wreckage almost at the peak of Cangshan but never had heard what it was. The meeting broke up on September 10, 2011, and MIA Recoveries headed for China to begin its search.

As soon as he arrived in China Clayton followed up with a trekking guide who had done some investigation of the mission even before Clayton left the U.S. The guide, Adam Kritzer, had visited several villages around Cangshan and had learned that a number of villagers remembered hearing of a crash high in the mountains during the war. He found seven locals who came from four different villages, but all knew of the crash and pinned the date to late 1942. He had hoped that one of these interviewees would lead him to the wreckage, but they declined. They said there was too much danger in such a climb.

Undeterred, Adam turned to another village, where he met a man who claimed his father had seen the crash while he was hunting and remembered that pieces were coming out of the plane just before it crashed. Other villagers said that in a 1977 hunting trip they found tin ingots in a stream close to the wreck. All these discussions made the objective that much clearer, and all led to the west side of Cangshan. The last group of villagers he interviewed, the ones whose father had seen the crash, finally agreed to lead Clayton up the mountain to the site.

Several days later the climbers set out through dense jungle at the bottom of the mountain, crossing a number of hazardous streams and beginning their tortuous climb. Here the guides stopped, then pointed to the crest of Cangshan, and quit. They said it was much too dangerous and headed back down the mountain. Clayton had no choice but to follow them down to the village. "I was stunned by their sudden and surprising refusal to proceed higher. I returned to Old Town Dali to regroup and reorganize," Clayton wrote later.

He found another tiny village on the west side of the target mountain, where a fifty-nine-year-old man told him that one day his father had been gathering medicinal herbs on the family hunting grounds high on the mountain. He noticed birds that seemed to be attacking prey of some kind, then noticed that there were three bodies, but the bones were too large to be the bones of Chinese. He looked further and found an airplane wing and parts of the fuselage. Over the years he took his sons to the location, the same sons that now became Clayton's guides.

Days later they started up the side of Cangshan, following pretty much the same path used earlier. Their first day went reasonably well, and they camped under some cave-like rock ledges, spending a cheerful night, looking forward to the possible discovery next day. Things went well until they came to the base of the high cliff on the summit. Presumably the wreckage lay in that area, but the rain came and his guides urged him to go back down the mountain before the rain turned the climbing area into a raging river. Clayton was deeply disappointed once again.

The force of the water made their descent to their base camp more than hazardous. As Clayton described it, "The steep, rocky drainage was now a flowing waterfall, making for probably my most dangerous down-climb of my entire mountaineering career." They made it to their base camp, which was under a rock overhang that provided some protection from the rain, but not the wind. They managed to build a large fire which they kept feeding all night, but two of the tents had washed away. There was no more dry firewood and they were out of food. The decision to go back to the village was not a hard one.

Back in the village, Clayton tried everything to get the guides to lead him when the weather cleared, but they had had enough and refused. At that point the weather forecast continued rainy days, so Clayton decided to shift to India to fulfill the other goal of his trip. He left on October 7 for Calcutta and a search for more lost Hump aircraft.

I was very unhappy that the first two searches had turned out badly, but Clayton had said he was not done and would give it another try when the weather permitted. He wrote me, "The good news is this, I feel this is most probably the site of #60. The next expedition will hopefully encounter better weather, and will give me adequate time to properly survey and excavate the site. . . . Hang in there, Bob, we will be successful!" Then he gave me other good news. A film director had heard about Clayton's search and wanted to see what he was doing. He turned out to be a really helpful friend, paid most of Clayton's expenses, and allowed MIA Recoveries to be less anxious about the need to control expenses. The film company made a number of offers, including putting him on staff for a period of time and paying for the change to his plane ticket. But they wanted him for a longer period than he felt he could manage, and India beckoned, with the hope of adding more closure to American families of the MIAs.

MIA Recoveries found two planes in India, a B-24 and a C-46, which made that part of his trip successful; however, Clayton had not given up on CNAC No. 60. In a separate issue, Diego Kusak, who had been such a help to him in research before the trip and had accompanied him in his first days in China, emailed me that Clayton was using CNAC money for his India journey, and that upset Diego. I knew that Clayton was dividing his trip, so I told him not to worry. However, he and Clayton never had a good relationship after that, until finally they had a complete blowup, and Diego departed the scene.

After reporting his new finds in India to JPAC, Clayton returned to Dali when the weather cleared to try once more to make a successful climb. He was fortunate to find the services of a guide from yet another village who claimed he had been to the site three times during the past ten years while he was on hunting trips looking for herbs to use in medicine. He not only was willing to make the ascent, but he found six porters who could carry new equipment Clayton had bought: a professional metal detector and an assortment of tools he hoped to use to dig for items the metal detector uncovered.

His guide surprised him by taking a different route than had been used in the two previous attempts. It turned out to be much longer, a four-day trek, but it avoided having to cross several of the rivers that became so dangerous when the weather turned nasty. He still had several rivers to cross, but they were reasonably tame compared to those on the September and October climbs. After four days of climbing and traversing they found their first evidences of a crash scene, bits of metal wreckage scattered over a fairly extensive field.

They established their base camp on a steep slope about one hundred yards from the site so they could cover the spread wreckage with more efficiency. Clayton mentioned that the high camp was "precariously" located near the crash site. He wrote me on November 24: "Plenty of smallish metallic wreckage was found on the ground surface or slightly below the surface. I did a very thorough search of the entire crash site area and approx. ¼ mi. down the rocky drainage channel. The metal detector continued to detect wreckage to almost ¼ mi below the spot where I believed impact occurred including some large/dense wreckage. The larger/denser wreckage detected could be engines or landing gear, but was too buried under boulders and rocky debris for me to effectively excavate with hand tools."

He further explained that in other wrecks heavier parts of the plane tended to wash down, with gravity as the accelerator, while small metal pieces often tend to get hung up on anything that projected from the natural path. It is known that a large earthquake took place in northern India in 1950, which could explain the boulders and rocky debris in the drainage paths. He had just experienced the heavy downpours causing the drainage areas to become violent rivers, so he understood the force the water could apply: even the heaviest objects could be moved by these rains.

The most amazing part of the discovery was that, of the many fragments and pieces of the plane that were exposed, one clearly showed the numbers 4681, which Clayton knew to be critical to the verification that this truly was the c-47 flown by John Dean and Jimmie Browne that had crashed so many years ago.

After so many years of effort, the news of the find was hard to digest. Verification did come when the Douglas Aircraft records showed that CNAC No. 60 had been assigned to CNAC on October 18, 1942, from the Indian Wing of the U.S. Air Corps. It also showed with finality the brief and tragic fate of the aircraft. But where was the crew? That mystery was yet to be solved.

The shattered carcass of the c-47 with construction number 4681, serial number 41-18556 lies buried under rocks and boulders turned loose probably by the violent earthquake of 1950. The wreckage is scattered over hundreds of feet, with a large number of aircraft pieces still visible. The piece that shows the construction number lies at N 25 38 58.7 and E 100 05 30.2 on grid maps. While much of the aircraft lies hidden under boulders, the metal detectors revealed that large pieces lie under the surface. The impact area is only a few miles from the city of Dali in Yunnan Province, a city situated at an elevation of six thousand feet.[1]

It appears that the aircraft hit Cangshan Mountain's 13,524-foot Malong Peak at about 13,400 feet. If they had been able to gain just two hundred feet more they might have cleared the peak and been safe. The mountain range has a series of peaks on the west side of Dali's Lake Erhai and is known for its botanical beauty and a number of ecological zones with a rich variety of plant species. It is a place of considerable beauty, with clouds screening many of its highest peaks and offering a variety of cloud formations. I visited there in 2015 and could see the peaks looking down on the ancient city of Dali and the long, blue Lake Erhai. It was peaceful and quiet until I found myself in the city center, with its busyness and noise. The city gates seem the same as they were hundreds of years ago, except for the modern vehicles passing through.

Today a cable car runs to the peak next to Malong Peak, ending at just over eleven thousand feet. Only one party has attempted to reach the wreckage using the cable car, when Hao Chen ventured from the platform down the valley and across the ridge to view the wreckage. He had hoped to descend the short distance to the wreck, but the weather suddenly shifted, and he was forced to give up and take the easy way down.

My son Tom and I took the same cable car to the 9,400-foot mid-station platform in September 2015 to at least glimpse the surroundings of the site, if not actually getting to the wreckage. It was some consolation, but not much.

# 18

The U.S. Army unit that was charged with the recovery and identification of MIAS was the Joint POW/MIA Accounting Command, whose operational center was at Hickam Field in Honolulu. After some controversy, in 2013 they became the Defense POW/MIA Accounting Agency, but the original mission remains the same:

> *OUR VISION* A world-class workforce fulfills our nation's obligation by maximizing the number of missing personnel accounted for while ensuring timely, accurate information is provided to their families.
>
> *OUR MISSION* To provide the fullest possible accounting for our missing personnel to their families and the nation.
>
> *OUR VALUES* Compassion: We conduct our work and communication with empathy. Integrity: We live our lives with truthfulness and objectivity. Teamwork: We are committed and willing to do all we can to assist each other, thereby strengthening our collective ability to partner with family organizations, veterans, public and private entities, foreign governments, and academia to achieve our mission. Respect: We always demonstrate the utmost regard for one another, our partners, and our missing personnel and their families. Innovation: We apply fresh thinking and continuously improve everyday.[1]

Before, we had been interested only in finding out more about CNAC and Jim's role, but as the years passed, we thought even more about the returning of his remains. I think Clayton turned me on to JPAC in about 2004 or so, and I began a lengthy correspondence with its rotating leadership. Unfortunately the leaders, appointed by the president and the chiefs of staff, are generally flag officers with just a few more years to serve and so sometimes do not feel a long-term commitment to success.

Although my initial dealings with JPAC were probably about 2004, I kept few records in the early years of our search, even as we began to get serious about our goals. One of my earliest documents is from Linda McFadyen, the U.S. State Department contact officer for our case. I had asked if any CNAC planes had been recovered, and in her July 5, 2006, response she said there had been no recoveries. In November 2006 I wrote the Defense POW/Missing Personnel Office (DPMO), the army agency overseeing JPAC, the following:

I have several questions which I have addressed to various agencies without results.

1) Is there a complete record anywhere of the number of aircrew still missing in the Hump (Himalayas) area from the 1942–1945 era?

2) Have there been recoveries of remains from that area in recent (ten) years?

3) Are there continuing searches or have searches for those missing ceased?

4) Is the DPMO interested in working with private expeditions seeking lost aircraft?

My cousin was a civilian so I have tried to work with the State Department's missing person's officer, but Jim was later declared a veteran so I contacted the Air Force and was referred to the Army since the Air Corps of 1942 was part of the Army, but I could get little information from anyone. JPAC, however, does research MIAs but only goes for the remains after someone locates them.

I sent copies of the letter to my senator, my congressman, the State Department, and the army and air force. There was only one answer to the letter, at least that is the only one that I can find. I know almost all the answers to all four questions now, but had no clue in 2006. Those answers are (1) no idea, (2) one, (3) never were any, (4) no.

My congressman then was Tom Feeney, now long gone. He sent a letter dated February 6, 2007, enclosing a copy of a letter from the army which said, "Inquiry into this matter has been initiated. You will be further advised as soon as information becomes available." That was the last I heard from that inquiry. Meanwhile, I had sought information directly from the army through a Freedom of Information Act request, asking for any information that they had on Jimmie. The army responded that they had found a James Browne, lieutenant, who was buried in Belgium. Even the army recognized that was not Jimmie. "We do not think this is the person for which you are seeking information," they wrote on June 5, 2007.

I also learned that JPAC was not the only agency involved with the still missing airmen. The DPMO was in most areas the supervisor of JPAC, and I further discovered that periodically DPMO/ JPAC would conduct briefings for MIA families. Usually there were six or seven held each year, altering locations in cities throughout the country. I heard from Linda McFadyen, who said that I could attend a briefing in Washington, DC, and the government would pay for the trip. But shortly afterward she contacted me again to say she had been mistaken, the briefing was only for Cold War and Korea MIAs, not for families of World War II veterans. Since the World War II MIAs number more than seventy thousand and the Korea and Cold War MIAs less than six thousand, I thought that odd. Some years later I was told that most cities could not find venues large enough for such a crowd. That also seemed odd.

After a DPMO briefing in Tampa, I wrote Senator Bill Nelson suggesting that families be notified of the discovery of all downed aircraft, even if the planes were not visited by JPAC. I received no answer. On May 21, 2007, I wrote Charles Ray, deputy assistant secretary of defense, about 73308, a C-47 that crashed in May 1946, carrying crew, passengers, and the remains of POWs who died in Japanese jails in Rangoon. No answer, but in this case families eventually were notified, probably by MIA Recoveries, and successfully lobbied for a JPAC mission.

I wrote again to Ray, this time asking that Jim's name be added to the DPMO database on MIAs from World War II. I am happy to say that that request was granted, and Jim is now listed with seventy-three thousand others on an obscure website on the DPMO (now DPAA) website. (This has been my sole victory in my skirmishes with DPAA and its predecessors.) On October 20, 2009, Ray resigned to become ambassador to Zimbabwe. Apparently much of his correspondence went with him.

In a chance encounter on a cruise to New Zealand in 2007, I had met Mike O'Brien, a retired major general from Australia, who had been involved in negotiations with India involving Australians buried in India. He was interested in our efforts, and those of Gary Zaetz and the *Hot as Hell* bomber. As soon as I came home, I emailed Johnie Webb, my contact from the DPMO briefing, asking him to get in touch with O'Brien, but Mike said later he never heard from anyone at DPMO or JPAC.

In 2010 there was another DPMO briefing, this time in Orlando. Donna and I went and met briefly with Dr. Ed Burton and Christine Cohn from DPMO. Christine mentioned that they were attempting to get permission to review the Taiwan archives, and I wondered if CNAC records survived there. She said she would look into it, but I have no record of further correspondence on the subject.

I left some questions with the DPMO staff, primarily devoted to the DPMO policy on searches for aircraft wrecks. I had read that the Chinese had issued a statement claiming that they now viewed searches for missing American airmen as a "bilateral humanitarian issue" and that "overall cooperation [was] cordial and productive." I was hoping to benefit from this new attitude.

Another area we felt had merit was the search of the Taiwan archives. Christine said she would find out if any archives were now open for U.S. research. That turned up a negative for any possible CNAC information.

In early 2012 I was contacted by Drew Speelhoffer of JPAC's history section, who promised that he would keep me informed of any new reports of Jim's case. He was interested in Clayton's findings and wanted to investigate them further. I corresponded for several months with Drew, but in mid-2013 I emailed him several times and I have never heard of him, or from him, since.

In the next few years I grew increasingly impatient, waiting for news that never came. The lack of communication from DPMO/JPAC; conversations with Gary Zaetz, whose uncle was on a B-24 that Clayton found and was having the same communications problems we were having; their treatment of Clayton; news clippings about the inefficiencies of JPAC; conversations with the Chinese embassy in Washington; word from the PLA in China; and word from Ken Tilley, a former DPMO employee—all this made me feel that there were things happening that I knew nothing about. I also knew I was one of many people trying to get information about loved ones missing during World War II, but because Jim was a civilian, not in the military, I believed that our case was different.

Then in 2013 several news sources reported that JPAC and DPMO were receiving scathing criticism of their activities, and this led to a Senate hearing on August 1, 2013. It had been reported that management at JPAC was inept and that present attitudes could lead from "dysfunction to total failure." The Senate committee criticized JPAC methods as "woefully inept and even corrupt" and accused personnel of wasting money on travel to the easy spots, Europe, for instance, and ignoring the tough areas.[2]

Senators Claire McCaskill and Kelly Ayotte were highly indignant that information about MIAs was not being given to the families. The hearing cited the fact that some forty thousand World War II MIAs were considered lost over water and were not recoverable. Those forty thousand are known by name and circumstances of death, but neither DPAA nor its predecessors had informed families that there was no possibility of recovery.

In the China-Burma-India theater at least twenty-two downed aircraft have been discovered and the names of the crews are known. Yet, to my knowledge, none of the families of the almost two hundred crew members has been notified by the army that their loved ones have been located. It does seem that the families should have some official notification of the MIA's location.

ENTER JPAC

That criticism of JPAC certainly sounded like music to my ears and maybe explained some of my treatment. But sadly, Congress's answer was to create a new agency, DPAA. Phone numbers stayed the same as under JPAC and the same desks were occupied by the same people. In time a new director was named, Lt. Gen. Michael Linnington, whom I respected. I looked forward to changes being made and the ship being tightened up, but he lasted only a few months before leaving to go to the Wounded Warrior Project. And the agency has certainly not improved its communications to families.

Congress seems to have its own set of troubles, so it is unlikely that any pressures will mount to make any other changes. In recent appointments, retired general Kelly McKeague is now heading DPAA after having been part of the leadership of JPAC in its troubled times. This no condemnation of the general, but a return of former leaders to the new agency does not give much confidence to the public that there is a serious effort to address the problems.

The new agency still has MIA Recoveries on its blacklist, so they are ignoring the man who knows the most about China-Burma-India and its MIAs. If there are no plans to use MIA Recoveries, then it probably makes little difference except to those who might benefit from his knowledge. In this case, DPAA seems to be a deterrent in reaching a successful conclusion to our mission. If, instead, Clayton were to be named a contractor for an excavation of CNAC No. 60, that might relieve the Chinese concerns about a U.S. military presence. But that is a moot point. My correspondence regarding CNAC No. 60 has been extensive over the years. The least productive of these efforts has been my attempts to interest DPAA in our case.

Periodically there are news articles that tell of an elected official's dedication to seeing a successful solution to a given military injustice. An award, a promotion, or recognition long overdue, but the people I have elected to represent me have shown no such dedication. Correspondence from Senator Bill Nelson is typical: "In response to my inquiry on your behalf, I am enclosing a copy of the correspondence I received from the. . . ." A letter written, a letter received, nothing more. I know that congressmen and senators have many duties and represent many people, but they also are our only link to bureaucracies that tower over the public.

Over the years I have attended four JPAC/DPMO briefings, but there is little reason to go when the answers are always the same. The Chinese won't let us in. Whatever skills are needed to convince the Chinese to honor pledges made to our government in 2008 to let searchers come into China on humanitarian missions, those skills are not available in the current DPAA. The same situation exists in India, which has not allowed searches on known American crash sites after one abortive attempt by JPAC.

Before the last briefing I attended I was told, I think by Linda McFadyen, that someone would be there from DPMO who would give me new material and have specific knowledge of the case, but I sat all by myself at a table for ten and only one person showed up, gave me a summary of Jim's history, and left. Much of the material in that history was information I had supplied. In all cases I tried to make Jim emerge as a person, with photos and descriptions of his quirky personality, but I finally realized that he was not a person to them; he was just another case, and we were a pain in the ass.

# PART 4

## THE PLOT THICKENS

# 19

## DPAA, PLA, and Me

Early in 2013 I wrote to JPAC asking several specific questions about a possible site investigation. I heard nothing from them, but my contact officer, Linda McFadyen, came to my assistance. I got her email in May 2013 with the answers to my questions, as set forth by JPAC. First, there would not be any investigations until 2014 due to workload. Second, they met with Chinese officials from the Ministry of Foreign Affairs in January 2013. Third, two other crash sites were presently being worked, both in Guangxi Province. More disappointing news.

In January 2014 I again emailed for information, and this time Johnie Webb replied promptly: "I understand your frustration concerning the case with your cousin lost in China. If I was in your position I know I would feel the same way you do." He went on to say no meetings with the Chinese were scheduled to discuss CNAC No. 60, but they were working to get one to discuss the sites in Yunnan Province. I emailed back suggesting that in the negotiations, they point out that Jim's plane was flying for a Chinese airline, with a Chinese radioman aboard, and crashed in China. I thought that might increase its priority with the Chinese. No response to that one.

I wrote again to Senator Nelson on July 10, 2013; in his diplomatic reply he forwarded DPMO's response that the search effort had not been scheduled. The letter to Nelson came from Gen. W.

Montague Winfield, who also said that JPAC planned to make a request to the Chinese during bilateral discussions, scheduled to occur in late 2013 or early 2014, to investigate the presumed crash site. The word "presumed" irritated me since the site had been reported and the aircraft identified, so there was no "presumption" of its existence. Later I wrote to my congressman, Bill Posey, as I had written his predecessor, but received no useful information.

It was in early 2014 that we first received notice that something might be breaking. Several years earlier I had seen an article that featured a meeting between a Flying Tiger organization and the People's Republic of China ambassador to the U.S. So I contacted the embassy by letter, introducing myself and explaining what my mission was. Shortly afterward I got a very nice email from Shiquan Wang, third secretary to the ambassador, asking if he could be of service. At the time, my emails from JPAC, when they bothered to reply, said only that nothing was happening for various reasons. Shortly before I wrote the embassy I had heard from our Chinese sources that the Peoples Liberation Army (PLA) was planning a meeting with JPAC to discuss China wreck sites. The meeting was to take place in 2013. I emailed JPAC asking for their news but, again, heard nothing.

By October 1, 2014, I was fuming, so I wrote to Linda at State asking for a Freedom of Information Act (FOIA) reply to my concerns. Being an FDIC retiree, I had once been required to answer banking FOIAs and knew it was a painful process. She said that she was working on the case. So I relented and told her, "Forget the FOIA and do what you can!"

Months earlier, at the end of 2013, I had called JPAC and was told by a staff sergeant that the meeting with the PLA had been postponed but would take place in May 2014. That staff sergeant was the most helpful person at JPAC I had run across. Then, on October 10, 2014, Linda replied to the email I had sent her in September. She had heard from Johnie Web at JPAC:

Finally I have some good news to share with you on Bob's case. Below is a short paragraph from the trip on the visit. The PLA investigated their first incident in Yunnan Province (JPAC 321 near Dali) and invited

JPAC to send a team to investigate in the province for the first time. This incident is the CNAC C-47 A/C that was presented to the PLA during our visit in Jan 2013. While in Yunnan, the PLA archivists spoke with many locals with knowledge of aircraft losses. The team did not visit the site due to difficulty of terrain but they believe we could reach site for operations.

I was a little disturbed by the fact that the news was a year and a half old, but it was very positive and raised our sagging hopes.

Unknown to me, in 2013 the PLA Archives team had investigated Jim's wreck site themselves, to see whether the request was legitimate. They spent some time in the Dali area interviewing, photographing, and measuring, but the weather was nasty and they never did make it to the actual site. However, they reported that the wreck could be approached with proper equipment, and they would assist in any way they could. There was no date on the PLA report, but later I learned it was written in early 2013.

After the October 10 email, I emailed Webb asking for a time line. He answered that it might be possible to add the search to a scheduled China visit in 2015. Even though the PLA had issued an invitation to JPAC to look for Jim's plane in 2013, by mid-2015 no real plan had been developed for the search.

We never saw that PLA report until a DPMO briefing that was held in Orlando in November 2014. My son Tom attended, as I was recovering from some minor surgery, and he saw the report and brought home the news that a search would take place by JPAC, who had now become DPAA, in August or September 2015. I contacted Secretary Shiquan Wang with that news, and he said he had heard the same news from his sources.

I kept emailing in 2015, and kept being reassured that the search was scheduled and would move ahead in that time frame. Then Wang emailed me that he had heard that a mission was actually scheduled for between July 2 and July 29. DPAA verified that, and for a few weeks I heard nothing more. Finally, I emailed Webb on June 11 and asked about the mission. He said it was still on schedule but cautioned that they would probably not get to the site, that the mission was an exploratory one to talk to villagers and determine what would be needed for the real search. They would send me a full report as soon as the team returned. That seemed to me to be redundant since the PLA had been there in 2014, and I doubt that anything had changed.

Then, on July 7, I sent another message and got back a bombshell. The mission had been scrubbed, no reschedule had been assigned, and it would probably not go until the next fiscal year, if at all. I was as much furious at the lack of communication, as I was disappointed. My only salvation was that DPAA had told me so many dates and facts that turned out not to be true, that I wasn't as shocked as I would have been if I had been dealing with a more reliable organization. I then fully understood all the nasty adjectives that were used by Congress in their investigation.

The only reason given for aborting the mission was that the PLA and local officials had not given permission for the U.S to send its search teams into Yunnan Province. I did not believe that was the reason. I believe there is some underlying reason, possibly because MIA Recoveries is involved. In a later email Webb said that he now knew that the scrub was because of the celebration of the seventieth anniversary of the end of World War II; because the personnel of all services were now devoted to that project, everything else would have to wait. Only a few days later a tremendous explosion in the port city of Tianjin meant a diversion of more troops to help that devastated area. And the term Webb used was "postponed," not "canceled." But that was little reassurance, as another delay could jeopardize future efforts.

# 20

---

## Beijing

---

An ironic twist came in an email from the Chinese embassy the day after that blow, asking me if I would accept an invitation to Beijing in August to see the celebration of the seventieth anniversary of the end of World War II. They would pay my expenses for a five-day stay, and it would give me a chance to meet with a representative of the PLA.

On July 8, the same day I received that invitation, I emailed Webb and other DPAA officials requesting a meeting with a PLA official while I was in Beijing. There was never any answer. At the same time I emailed Secretary Shiquan Wang asking for the same thing. He promptly replied that he would see what he could do.

On July 19 I wrote again to Linda: "Still not a word from DPAA, I expect they have written me off in some military fashion." Her reply was to say that she had forwarded an email to me four days before and that was considered word from DPAA. She seemed to be indicating that I was criticizing DPAA unfairly. Johnie Webb told her that cancelation of this particular mission was the sole decision of the Chinese, and that he would provide more information when he returned to the office. He said that DPAA would continue to press the Chinese to allow the U.S. military to conduct the investigation as planned. But not a word to me from DPAA. His reply to Linda was typical: we'll get back to you. Sometimes he did, but many times he failed to.

The next day I emailed Linda again and asked her to see if she could get me a PLA meeting. On July 21 she wrote that her contacts at the U.S. embassy in Beijing said they had never dealt with the PLA and didn't think the PLA would ever accept an inquiry from us, but they hoped we would get some cooperation from Chinese officials. She ended, "I tried." I responded that she seemed to be the only one who was trying, and she emailed right back that there actually had been a DPAA team that was ready to go, so they were really trying. That gave me some reassurance that DPAA was truly planning to move forward.

Again I turned to Wang, thanking him for my Beijing invitation. As a sidelight, at my grandson's baseball game on July 11, my son Tom had casually asked if I needed company on my China trip. Of course, I said. So on Monday I emailed Eric, my trip coordinator at the Washington Chinese embassy, to see if Tom could come with me. Eric emailed back on the 14th that Tom was approved; I would fly business class and they would give Tom an economy ticket. It seemed that we were being blindsided by the Chinese on the search but warmly welcomed to the celebration. That seems to be the way governments work.

In my email to Wang, I ended, "I guess my deep disgust right now is the disrespect we are showing these three fliers, one Chinese, two Americans by allowing their remains to lie on a hilltop, not getting the respect and the dignity of a proper burial. And we know where they are!" He emailed right back that he completely understood my feelings and he had been trying to learn what the problem was. He assured me that the Chinese had no reason to show disrespect to the friends who sacrificed for them. And then he asked for more time to search for answers to the refusal to allow a search.

The next day he wrote that Jim and all heroes who helped China in the war deserved all the respect that China could show. He added that it was his real pleasure to help a "hero's family like yours." But he went on to say he had not heard back from Beijing and so he had asked a friend in the PLA to check. That friend told him that the PLA hadn't refused the request from the U.S. No other details. Still, the U.S. Chinese embassy people were waiting for a formal response from Beijing.

On July 23, Angie Chen, a CNAC member who lives in Guangzhou, emailed that she had a friend at the PLA in Beijing and asked for permission to call her for information. I of course agreed to it. On the 25th Angie reported her conversation with Colonel Liu of the PLA, who said the embassy was right, that the PLA had not refused entry; she believed that local officials were barring the way. Angie has asked Liu if I could meet with someone from the PLA on September 2 during my stay in Beijing. I sent Angie a copy of the email invitation to forward to the colonel since the formal invitation had not yet arrived.

Tom and I continued to prepare for the visit: applying for a Chinese visa, preparing a medical statement and a list of medications, writing a brief biography to be used for our introduction, and so on. We were to fly to Beijing, take part in the three events during the September 3 celebration, then head back to Orlando on the 4th. Since it was such a long trip for such a short stay, I asked if we could visit Dali and maybe ride the cable car to a peak of the Cangshan Mountain and get as close as possible to Jim. That seemed to be okay with the powers that be, and they came back with two possible side trips, one to Nanjing to see the Monument to the Aviator Martyrs in the War of Resistance against Japanese Aggression and Museum or to Yunnan and Dali. We chose Dali since Cangshan Mountain was kind of our shrine.

Then the Chinese questioned whether I, at age eighty-nine, was able to physically make the Yunnan trip. Dali is at an elevation of roughly six thousand feet and the cable car ascends to about eleven thousand, and they worried about my advanced age. They asked me to get permission from my doctor, but he refused, saying he wouldn't give me written permission to play bingo.

A few days later the Chinese sent our tentative transpacific tickets, along with a request for a list of my pills, major surgeries, and major physical problems, and a general statement about my old carcass. Our final tickets and itinerary arrived just five days before departure, but still there was nothing about Dali and when we would return to Beijing. Then they said they could route us through Shanghai, much closer to Dali. But the following day I got a message that a new flight was scheduled for us out of Beijing. The new plan was for us to fly from Beijing to Dali, spend a few days there, then go on to Nanjing to the Monument to the Aviator Martyrs for two days, then take the bullet train to Shanghai for our return to San Francisco. I had planned to go to San Francisco after the China trip for the four-day CNAC reunion, so the change worked out very well. I could not have asked for better destinations.

However, with the change of plans, and the Tianjin explosion, all hopes of meeting with the PLA evaporated. Webb now told me that the minister of foreign affairs, not the PLA or the local folks, had given the order to call off the search. I knew then that any effort to speak with the PLA was unnecessary.

Our flight from Detroit to Beijing was long. I had a business-class seat with a coffin-like arrangement so I could lie down, but since I think the engine was no more than three feet from my head, I managed very little rest. We had arranged it so that Tom was in the first row of economy and I was in the last row of business, so we were separated only by a curtain through which I could easily transit with beverages in hand.

When we arrived in Beijing, we were given the VIP treatment. As we exited the plane we were met by a quartet of uniformed young ladies plus Wu, who would be our translator/guide and protector throughout our stay. Next we were escorted to a lounge while we waited for our passports to go through immigration and our bags to be collected. We were even more impressed when we were given our room keys on the way to the hotel. No checking in, no credit card, no ID, just walk toward the elevator and let yourself in—bags will follow.

They gave us a new schedule for our time after Beijing, which gave us two days in Dali, then to Nanjing, and a home flight from Shanghai. All made good sense, and we went to bed in the Grand Hyatt Hotel, just two blocks from Tiananmen Square. The whole area was under strict security, so there was no temptation to wander around.

The main reason for the trip was to attend the events of September 3, which were to be held on our third day in town. But before that we were taken to the Civil Aviation Museum. It was our request that we see the new museum that Angie Chen had spent so much time and effort to promote. It was in a huge hangar-type building out by the airport. Wu escorted us in our Mercedes limo right to the main entrance. Everything in Beijing, including the museum was closed in preparation for the big parade the next day. But Angie had made sure that we could see the museum and its CNAC exhibit, so the museum staff director and his assistant greeted us and showed us around.

Most of the open space was taken up with aircraft of different eras, sizes, and types. Fixed-wing and rotor-driven models were on display, and narratives were presented in both English and Chinese, so the tour was entertaining as well as educational. Outside was a khaki-colored C-47, a C-46, and a rather plain old DC-3. Tucked away in one corner of the museum itself was the CNAC exhibit, which was great. There were lots of photographs, articles, and two well-done tablets that listed CNAC flight personnel and those who died while serving China. Interestingly, much of the CNAC display featured the final days of CNAC and the defection of CNAC Chinese leadership with eleven CNAC and Central Air Transport planes to the Communists in Peking. Of course, to the Communists these were not defections but a rush to join the new government. The exhibit was well done and paid homage to the old hands even though they were part of the despised Chiang Kai-shek era. CNAC No. 60 was featured as the first Hump fatality, and Angie had very nicely added my name to the plaque as a contributor of the names, dates, and places of some of the fatal crashes.

September 3 dawned cloudless and beautiful, a perfect day for the incredible parade that took place. The precision of every unit was a marvel: infantry in perfect step, trucks and vehicles lined up with bumpers perfectly in line, and the officers who barked out the commands executing their salutes with real perfection. It was a wonderful sight.

Immediately after the last flyover with multicolored jet streams, we boarded buses to go across Tiananmen Square to the Great Hall of the People for a special, intimate lunch for 748 people. There were a few brief speeches that were translated on individual headsets. The meal was served by hundreds of young students from Beijing schools. A very decent meal for that many people.

And we did get to see President Xi Jinping from a distance. He sat stiffly at the head table and made brief remarks, efficiently translated. While it was not the cozy, friendly, lunch we thought we might share with some officials, it was a good example of Chinese efficiency.

After that it was back to the hotel for a rest. We had been invited to an evening event, but it was touted as a loud, noisy, crowded cultural event, so I talked Tom out of going since we had to be up at 3:30 a.m. to get to a 6:20 flight. We made it with many a yawn, and they still had me in business class, where I was the sole occupant and was served a fine breakfast. The flight took us along part of the Himalayas, where cloud cover hid all but the highest peaks. But with a bright blue sky, the solid bank of clouds, and the snow-covered peaks of the world's highest mountain range poking through, I could not have been happier.

The beauty of a 6:10 a.m. flight is that we were in Dali ready for a full day's activities by 10:30. Again our room keys were in the limo, so we just walked through the lobby and were escorted to our Regent Hotel rooms in the Ancient City. Our rooms were palatial, with a gigantic bed in one room and a sitting area with several leather couches and a fully stocked desk and computer. Sadly, the computer was in Chinese, and our internet did not work.

After we checked in we left for lunch at a small inn off a back road with a couple of auto repair garages for neighbors. It was our first real Chinese meal; few people spoke English, and all dishes were passed on a lazy Susan. I had a beef dish that was good and not spicy. Dessert was noodles. Conversation turned to the AVG Flying Tigers. As was usual, the Chinese figured any American flier in China during World War II was a Flying Tiger. Tom and I were therefore recognized as relatives of a Tiger. As many times as we explained that we really were not Tigers, it had no effect.

One of our party had written a book about Flying Tigers at the Salween River, probably the group's finest hour. It was at the Salween River Bridge in early May 1942 that the AVG sortied time after time through the narrow Salween gorge and drove back for good the Japanese troops attempting to come into China's southwest. This gentleman had a copy of his book with him, which he presented to me. I promised him a copy of my book, which I retrieved from the hotel and later gave to him. I doubt that the exchange benefited either of us since his was in Chinese, and mine was in English. But the gesture was well meant.

Then we took off for Cangshan Mountain. Over some rugged, torn-up, miserable roads we finally ended up at the cable car station. As we approached the landing, a group of fifteen or twenty people was waiting for us. Most of them wanted to have their photos taken with me or Tom, but one lady approached with a large bouquet of yellow flowers. I asked Wu what they were for and she said it was to honor Jim and his crew. I asked what I should do with them and she said, "Just follow the lady with the flowers!" So Tom and I followed her through a door, up two flights of stairs to another door, which opened right onto the cable cars, which slowly approached. An attendant opened the door of one and motioned us in, so Tom and I, the flower lady, and a man began our upward climb. (Later we found out he was a medic carrying a defibrillator, just in case I should need reviving.)

We reached the halfway station at 9,400 feet and left the car. I was still wondering just what came next, when the flower lady handed me the bouquet, and Wu, who had been right behind us, walked me over to the corner of the platform and suggested I place the flowers facing the slope of Malong Peak, in the direction of the wreckage. I finally realized that I could spend a few moments of silence as a kind of homage to Jim, John Dean, and K. L. Yang. The rest of the group stood back respectfully as I formed a few thoughts and placed the bouquet in the corner.

As casually, as suddenly, as this had developed, it was still very emotional for me, but as I saw in the Chinese faces around me, they felt the impact as well. Many had had no idea that Americans had died for China on their mountain, in their backyard, until Tom and I arrived. There were some misty eyes as I turned away, and two of them were mine. As I stood there I realized that, with the hostility of the agencies involved, this was probably the only funeral service those three aviators would ever have. I felt a sense of outrage that the bureaucrats of the world could rob them of the chance to receive the honors and respect to which they were entitled. I felt a renewed determination to do what I could to allow them some form of finality and recognition.

Both of us had pleaded with Wu to let us relax and have a simple dinner at the hotel, but instead we were loaded on our minibus and taken to a nearby restaurant, where we were paraded to a small room in the back. Included in our entourage were five or six people whose specific duties were unknown to us but who appeared regularly at our various destinations. Sometimes very visible, mostly not, they were responsible for the myriad details of our stay and did a magnificent job.

During the ride back to the hotel, and later at the hotel, Tom and I mused about the day. He was as puzzled about the events of the day as I was, but both of us felt we had accomplished something significant. I wished that all MIAs could have such a moment. It was a day that we will both long remember.

The rest of our stay in Dali was a tourist's delight. It was pure fun: a lavish breakfast at the hotel, then a bus ride to the dock of a multideck lake steamer for a cruise on Lake Erhai. We had a room with a balcony for incredible views of Cangshan and its eleven peaks, and we visited two islands in the lake, both scenic, historic, and crowded. On the boat, we were treated to a show by local performers in full, colorful dress. Afterward we had photos taken with the ladies, but we never were able to see the results. After our cruise we visited Dali's most famous landmark, the Three Pagodas, and completed our tour of the city.

That night we had dinner at a magnificent city hall with a number of local dignitaries, complete with myriad toasts and a number of gifts, primarily books about Dali and Yunnan Province. Dinner was traditional Chinese, and my chopsticks defied me once again, while Tom mastered his with ease. As usual I ended up with one of China's few forks.

In later correspondence I was told that it was local officials from Dali and Yunnan that were opposed to our search, but that night they were congenial and entertaining, and Wu was the center of bilingual efforts. A good evening and a lovely building and setting at the very foot of Lake Erhai.

Next morning, September 6, a Sunday, we left for Nanjing. Originally we were to have a nonstop flight to Shanghai, then take a bullet train to Nanjing and back, but that flight was overbooked, so we settled for a flight from Dali to Kunming, then another flight on another airline to Nanjing. As had been the case in every other flight, I was up front in business and Tom and Wu followed in steerage. I had a great breakfast on the flight to Kunming, while Tom and Wu had tea. I had a tasty lunch on the Nanjing plane, and Tom and Wu had tea.

In Kunming, Wu and Tom had met several minor crises getting our airline switch accomplished, with security, baggage, and time causing them some anxious moments. As they were struggling with logistics, I was relaxing in a VIP room, remembering the previous visit to the airport in 2010. Then it had a single runway and a single terminal building, but now it had several additional runways and three terminal buildings. Wu and Tom finally mastered the details and we arrived somewhat late in Nanjing. We were met by a minivan and hustled to the splendid Jinling Hotel, where Tom and I shared a room on the forty-sixth floor, our only shared accommodation on the trip. The hotel exuded class and elegance; our breakfast on the fifty-sixth floor overlooked downtown Nanjing, with the Yangtze River in the distance.

At dinner with the Friendship Committee of Jiangsu Province we met the deputy secretary of the Jiangsu People's Association for Friendship for Foreign Countries, Duan Haihong, who looked more like my granddaughter's college roommate than an executive. Her organization had been in charge of our trip from the beginning, some of it done by the Washington office, some by the Beijing headquarters, and this part by the local Nanjing office. I was glad to learn more about its existence and to establish contact with its people. We had another "simple" thirteen-course lazy-Susan meal, but with education as a side dish.

The next day began well as we headed for the western section of Nanjing and the Monument to the Aviation Martyrs. We were met there by several staff members and visited briefly in front of the museum, a great glass cube-like structure with a golden archer mounted on what could have been a flying tiger. It was a striking entrance to the grounds of the museum and the path to the monument, up some two hundred steps. We were asked what we wanted to see; I suggested the museum and the CNAC exhibit, since we had donated several articles after we visited in 2010. But we were told that the CNAC things were presently in storage. That seemed a bit strange, but museums do switch exhibits from time to time.

With that in mind we began our trip up the path to the monument. We got about halfway there, with some one hundred steps still to go, when I called it quits and asked Tom to photograph the monument and the inscription of Jim's name on the black marble stone. Tom had no trouble navigating, nor did Wu, for which I was grateful. I made my descent with Tom's help; open stairs with no railings defeat me, but with his shoulder to stabilize me, I doddered on down.

At the foot of the monument's hill, our host said that in order to make it to lunch and a timely arrival at the train station, we would have to leave without seeing the museum. Our failure to see the museum was a double blow, since I had been asked to give a talk at the CNAC reunion on my way home, and part of the presentation was to report on the museums in both Nanjing and Beijing. So it was with some disappointment that we boarded our bus for the forty-five-minute ride to a modest hotel where lunch had been set up for us in a VIP room with just five of us, including the bus driver. As usual, we were provided a very good Chinese, lazy-Susan-type meal that had some delicious shrimp. I mastered the chopsticks easily for two shrimp, but finally asked for the more familiar fork.

Tom was eager to ride the bullet train to Shanghai, his first train trip at the ripe old age of fifty-six! From lunch to the train station took another forty-five minutes, and we looked with some longing at the McDonald's directly across from the train terminal. Had we eaten there we would have been able to spend at least an hour at the museum. No matter, we were dropped off with all our luggage at the VIP Hall of Nanjing's enormous train station for our 1:00 p.m. bullet train departure. Off the very elegant VIP Hall were several small VIP rooms with comfortable chairs and the ever-present tea. Soon a young lady ushered us onto the station platform right by the trains. Unfortunately, the bullet train was farthest from the VIP room, and we had forgotten what a chore luggage could be, but we hastened down the corridor to the escalator and down to the train. All the time we were watching the clock tick up toward 1:00 and seeing the distance we had yet to go. It is no surprise that we did make it, but not comfortably. We were in the very first car, in the train's business class, which had only five airline-type chairs that could move to the completely flat position. It was a remarkable trip that took one hour and thirty-seven minutes.

Here was our only failure in transportation punctuality. We left the train in the Shanghai station and went out the large exit tunnel, pulling and carrying our luggage up the incline to street level. There we waited for our van, and waited. Wu called the driver only to find out he was at the wrong station, some forty-five minutes away. There were no seats, so we sat on our suitcases until they flattened out, then stood, waiting impatiently. Eventually the familiar minibus arrived and took us miles away from the hotel center and the Bund area, to a suburban-like setting in a residential subdivision. There three hotel buildings, just two stories high, accepted guests on a luxurious scale. It was the Hong Qiao State Guest House, one of the finest hotels anywhere.

The manager of our unit met us in a tux, with five staff members in uniform at his side. He presented me with a bouquet of red flowers that were both handsome and fragrant, then showed us to our rooms, for which we already had keys. We had only an hour before it was dinner time, and this time we could choose where to eat. They took us to a small area with a mix of American, Italian, Chinese (of course!), and Greek food. We chose Greek and had a quick meal, then went back to the Guest House.

Tom and I had been working on a visual program for my CNAC reunion in San Francisco, and now we struggled with downloading pictures from two cameras, selecting the ones we wanted to use, then making a new folder for those selected, and finally creating a flash drive ready for show. I say "we," but Tom was by far the mastermind, and it was his product that gave my presentation the spark it needed. When that was accomplished we celebrated by raiding the minibar. Strangely, that 50 yuan charge was the only bill we paid on the entire trip. Less than $10.

We walked over to the main hotel unit to have breakfast on the morning of September 8, accompanied by the hotel manager, who must have feared for my well-being on the twenty-yard walk. Breakfast was plentiful, and then we were shepherded by another staff member back to our unit. From there we were taken to Shanghai's airport and our flight home. The bus drove up to the VIP entrance similar to the train depot, and we were escorted to a small VIP room, where we were given back our passports and boarding passes. At 12:10 we boarded a bus and were driven across the tarmac to our United 747. We left the bus by the plane and climbed two flights of stairs to find ourselves at the door of the plane. We separated, Tom and I, as we boarded; I went upstairs and Tom went to the back of the economy section. The less said about the flight for either of us, the better.

And just like that it was over. From then on we had to handle our own bags, tickets, boarding passes, meals, and lodging, and adapt to the strain of VIP-less life. Tom went on to Orlando, while I stayed in San Francisco for two days of CNAC reunion and two days with daughter Barbara, who flew down from Portland. The reunion was great, and it was good to see some familiar faces after missing the last few get-togethers. But I was ready to go home.

# 21

## The Next Step

The CNAC reunion gave me some additional information in the form of a fellow presenter, Hao Chen from Seattle. After my turn at the podium, I was approached by Hao and his friend Fan. Hao said he wanted to show me some parts of a documentary he was working on, about the AVG, and particularly John Dean. He had been researching the crash of CNAC No. 60 from Dean's perspective. I did not get to hear his presentation because my daughter Barbara had flown in from Portland, and we were to spend the brief two-day visit together. Hao offered to come to my room and show me what he had shown at the reunion, so we agreed to meet at 8:30 that night.

Hao had been on Malong Peak in Dali recently, but never made it to the wreckage due to heavy rains. There he had met villagers who were part of a burial party of the three pilots. Now he was planning to fly from Kunming to the Dinjan area in a reconstructed DC-3. His documentary was to include as much as possible about the two American pilots, and he wanted my help. Roy Dean, John's brother, had met with Hao at an AVG reunion and was interested in the project. My contacts with Roy had been pleasant but not productive.

I was puzzled that I had not been aware of Hao's project before this. When I checked with Angie Chen, the CNAC Association member living in China, who had met him briefly, she said that he had presented the idea of the DC-3 crossing, then flying the airplane to various Chinese aviation locations and afterward presenting the plane to the Beijing Civil Aviation Museum. He had requested a substantial sum to make the flights feasible but was turned down. Still, I thought, anyone who shows interest in any phase of the CNAC No. 60's fate is a friend.

A number of factors now played into any further investigation of CNAC No. 60:

1. Hao Chen was told that the bodies of the three airmen had been wrapped in GI blankets and buried near the airplane. Bodies and plane were badly burned. The site of the burial was a flat spot near the plane and supposedly could be easily examined.

2. The locals, over a period of time, had cut up most of the main part of the plane and its outer skin and taken it to the villages to be either sold or made into useful tools.

3. Given the present antagonism between the U.S. and China, there was little chance that DPAA, being a part of the U.S. Army, would be permitted to enter China to examine the site.

4. The site appeared to be much more approachable than in the past, thanks to the cable car that goes to roughly twelve thousand feet.

Based on these four factors, I believed three questions remained:

1. Would it be feasible to have DPAA hire MIA Recoveries to recover remains and turn them over to DPAA for identification?

2. Would it be possible to create our own search effort exclusive of DPAA interests?

3. In the worst case, could we abandon the attempt to bring remains home and simply place a memorial at a suitable location? I believed a memorial would be appropriate even if we removed the bodies because China needed more visible signs of CNAC's sacrifices.

I began to think of a less dramatic end to our quest. Given the circumstances that exist in the political contest between China and the U.S., there is the fact that the Chinese are reluctant to have

U.S. Army units in their country. There may be minor exceptions to that concern, but DPAA becomes a very high-visibility presence in any search area, and this is a problem for the Chinese government. It is possible, however, that a smaller, private organization might be able to get to the site and search for remains without disturbing the politics of the day. I thought of MIA Recoveries.

In the months that followed the China trip, a few other developments offered some rays of sunshine. First, Angie was involved with a number of museums that included space for CNAC. The Nanjing Monument to the Aviator Martyrs in the War of Resistance against Japanese Aggression and its museum had been a pet project of hers for some time, and the Civil Aviation Museum in Beijing had included several displays of CNAC materials, photographs, and plaques. In these dealings Angie had become respected as both knowledgeable and available. She and I had developed a chart of CNAC war casualties, both American and Chinese, and that had been converted into a handsome metal plaque at the Civil Aviation Museum.

In her various activities she had met a number of Chinese who were interested in World War II and aviation, and some of these were men with considerable wealth. One was Fan Jianchuan, a historian who for years has collected artifacts for his private museum in Chengdu.

Angie had kept in touch with Colonel Liu of the PLA Archives Section, who suggested that the Jianchuan Museum might be interested in CNAC No. 60 and urged her to pursue the idea. Fan had been largely responsible for recovering a C-87 air corps transport that had been lost in Tibet in 1943, finding the wreckage pretty well preserved by the icy Tibetan winters. Chinese newspapers reported the find in August 2015: "Wreckage of an air freighter that was navigating over the Hump, the name given by Allied World War II pilots to the eastern part of the Himalayas due to the difficult challenge the mountain range posed to the pilots, when it crashed into a glacier 70 years ago and where its debris have since remained, was moved from Bomi County, Tibet, to Chengdu, Sichuan province on August 11. The valuable historical relics which are an important part of the story of Sino-U.S.

cooperation during WWII will be sent to China's largest private museum, Jianchuan Museum."[1]

It looked as if the Jianchuan Museum might be the knight in shining armor that could do what the U.S. and China could not. Angie made contact with staff of the museum and gave them the particulars of our unique flight: Chinese airline, mixed Chinese and American crew, and a location inside China. Months later a brief reply explained that the Tibetan experience had been more expensive than anticipated, and there were two other wrecks ahead of us. We recognized another dry well and looked again to DPAA.

To keep our options open, I emailed the U.S. State Department and DPAA asking how firm the 2016 date was and whether it was actually in the DPAA schedule. They confirmed that there was a mission planned for China during the August–September timeframe. Webb said he needed to check with the desk officer to see which sites had been approved by the Chinese for us to visit. That was a surprise, since the PLA had expended much time and energy in their 2013 search and had ended with a pledge to support a U.S. effort.

As an added thought, I contacted the Veterans Administration cemeteries section to ask about possible markers to be placed in China. I was so impressed by my visit to Cangshan that I thought there should be some way that Jimmie's sacrifice should be acknowledged in China. The beauty of the area, with the lake below and the city of 9 million people stretched along its shores, captured by the magnificent mountain ranges, seemed a happy alternative to our goal—still the recovery of the crew's remains.

The answer was a request for more information since Jim was a civilian pilot, hired by the Pan Am affiliate. We sent a three-page summary of his status, prepared by the Department of Defense, his death certificate, and a CNAC report of the accident. Then we waited for a reply. It was a rather unique application, but we believed it fell within the guidelines of the Department of Veterans Affairs. The only variation we suggested was that it be written in two languages, English and Chinese.

It was our hope to place a marker at the same spot where I had placed the pretty yellow flowers in September 2015, at the corner of the cable car platform 9,400 feet up the north slope of Cangshan Mountain. The dilemma was that, if we were successful in having a U.S. government memorial placed in China, we could not get a U.S. government gravestone for him if the DPAA search found his remains. Given the current state of DPAA, the Chinese government, and the laborious identification process, the Chinese marker might be more satisfactory to our family. However, that request was never answered, so apparently no marker will be placed in Dali.

An email from Webb on January 12, 2016, pledged that DPAA had scheduled the dates of August 14 to September 20, 2016, for the mission, pending Chinese approval. That approval would have to come from the minister of foreign affairs himself. Later Webb emailed that a meeting with the Chinese would take place in February, and Jim's case would be discussed once again.

With that information, I emailed Shiquan Wang at the Washington embassy asking him to verify the information. He promptly emailed back that the minister of foreign affairs was going to be in Washington "soon," and Wang would be included in the meetings. He assured me that when he saw the ministry officials, he would express my concerns to them, and I was sure that he would.

The next few months gave us some time to review where we were and what we really wanted to accomplish. Our original goal remained the same, to bring Jim home, but certain factors had come to pass that made that goal seem less than realistic. Having found the wreck site, and knowing what it was like, we now believed a final resting place on Cangshan would be a very satisfying end to our quest. Clayton's description of the conditions surrounding the plane made a successful recovery even less likely, and the political games played by both DPAA and the Chinese seemed to create perpetual roadblocks. All these factors pushed us toward a decision to end the project on Cangshan, create some memorial in China, and declare success.

Still, the nagging that had propelled us to this point was still there. Knowing that a search was scheduled, although still waiting for Chinese permission, indicated the U.S. government's continuing interest, and we felt that after years of prodding JPAC, DPAA, DPMO, and other agencies, giving up just did not seem right. So, without any formal discussion, we kept on, with the added mission of creating a memorial plaque in China describing the two Americans and one Chinese who gave their young lives to help the beleaguered nation.

Our new resolve crashed on February 24, 2016, when we received the following email from DPAA:

CLASSIFICATION: UNCLASSIFIED

CAVEAT: None

Hello Bob,

DPAA hosted Chinese officials from the [Ministry of Foreign Affairs] and the PLA Archives earlier this month and the loss of CNAC 60 (Incident 321-A) was discussed.

The PLA Archivists provided an update on their investigation into this loss during joint talks conducted in Beijing during September 2014. Their research findings concluded that the crash site of the aircraft was located on the southern slope of Malong peak in the Cang Shan mountains near Dali (Yunnan Province) at an altitude of approximately 12,000 feet. The PLA Archivists did not attempt to access the crash site during the course of their investigation due to the altitude and rugged terrain which is extremely dangerous. DPAA formally requested permission to conduct a joint research investigation of this incident and two other cases during 2015, but unfortunately local officials in Yunnan Province refused our access request.

During the bilateral talks held on 1 February, Chinese officials strongly recommended that CNAC 60 and the two other Yunnan incidents recommended for joint investigation during 2015 be closed for further investigation. Chinese officials advised investigation of CNAC 60 was too dangerous for further pursuit with access to the crash site location requiring a 15-day ascent with skilled mountaineers. Based on this recommendation, DPAA requested assistance from the Chinese to obtain additional photographic documentation of the area for the families if possible. The Chinese advised they would consider partnering opportunities with mountaineering groups in the area who may be able to access the mountain. DPAA will continue to discuss and follow-up on this option with the Chinese during 2016.

Bob, I know this is not the information you wanted to receive but it lays out where we are with the CNAC 60 crash site today. I will be happy to answer any questions you might have concerning the above information.

Respectfully,
Johnie E. Webb, Jr.

That was a serious blow to our hopes, and very depressing. Several questions to Webb went unanswered, as had two letters sent to DPAA head Michael Linnington. After we had digested the content of the email, we turned to the thought that the Chinese might consider partnering with the private sector. We felt this was an open invitation to insert MIA Recoveries into the mix. After all, Clayton had discovered the wreckage initially, knew the site and its hazards, and had recruited locals to make the ascents to the site in 2011. With that in mind, Clayton sent DPAA a proposal to search the site.

I joined them in urging permission for a project that would seem to answer everyone's objections and concerns. But there was no answer to either my input or Clayton's proposal. Several other MIA Recoveries proposals had been previously sent to DPAA, but DPAA had never replied, so their lack of interest was no surprise.

When Tom and I were in China visiting Dali, we were honored with a dinner that included Dali officials and treated with great respect. We were given books on Dali and its geography, as well as its history. We also felt a warm feeling toward the local residents of the city who, with little planning or advance knowledge, escorted us to the cable car and rose with us to the 9,400-foot platform and shared with us the moment as we placed the flowers in tribute to the crew of CNAC 60. We had no inkling that anyone in Dali would protest the arrival of a search team.

I still get misty-eyed when I remember my feelings on that cable car platform. So it was hard for me to believe that it was locals who were objecting to our search, although it does reinforce the idea that the protest was a political decision made at the highest levels. It may have been true that the Chinese were concerned about a U.S. military unit of any kind entering the country. If that was the case, any further push on government agencies here or there would have been useless.

Meanwhile, Clayton had been communicating with Keith Phillips, a forensic anthropologist from the University of Illinois who had indicated an interest in being part of a DPAA search. Keith had been working to obtain contract work for the university's Archaeology and Anthropology Department, and had brought MIA Recoveries, Inc. into the discussions.

In 2015 Clayton resubmitted several proposals to include the university, and even spelled out that the principal investigator in archaeology would be a graduate student from the university. At that point there seemed to be no interest on the part of DPAA in outsourcing work for China-Burma-India recoveries.

Then on March 8, 2016, I received an email from Webb at DPAA in response to an inquiry I had sent concerning an MIA proposal that had included University of Illinois personnel.:

CLASSIFICATION: UNCLASSIFIED

CAVEAT: None

Dear Bob,

Thank you for sharing this with me. The Director of our Strategic Partnership reached out to the University of Illinois at Chicago to see what their relationship is with Mr. Kuhles. We are working a partnership with the university; however, they have informed us that they have no current or planned dealings with Mr. Kuhles.

When I forwarded the email to Clayton, he replied by describing specific conversations with John Monaghan and others at the university. I emailed Dr. Monaghan to get some clarification, and he repeated that before the university would participate, they needed assurance that both the Ministry of Foreign Affairs and the PLA had approved the plan. We were back to the Chinese roadblock.

In April 2016 I emailed Webb at DPAA and Linda McFadyen at the State Department to ask if there were any scheduled meetings with the Ministry of Foreign Affairs, but I heard nothing back. At this time relations between the Chinese government and the U.S. were under considerable strain. China had suffered several economic slowdowns that destabilized both their markets and their currency. Territorial disputes with Japan over the northern Pacific Kuril Islands forced the U.S. to back Japan, and continuing pressure to see better human relations in China kept the pot boiling. These were major factors in the lack of cooperation in our mission.

Clayton and I began to look at another way to get to CNAC No. 60. We believed that if we could somehow arrange a purely private venture, ignoring both militaries, we might be able to quietly send a team to Dali and inconspicuously arrive at the crash scene. That might take the matter out of the political arena and switch it to a humanitarian effort. Of course, there were a few minor details, such as funding and timing, but it was worth a new effort since nothing else was in the works. I emailed a brief outline of the plan to Shiquan Wang. His reply was somewhat encouraging, and he promised to investigate.

Several weeks passed with no news from either camp, so I emailed Shiquan again, with no result. Nothing came from Webb, either, so I contacted DPAA to see what was going on. Still no word. Finally, I decided to go to Washington and sit down with Shiquan and Clayton. My daughter had just moved into her new job with the Red Cross and was staying with a friend in Wheaton, Maryland, so I asked her to join us. I got an immediate response from Shiquan, agreeing to meet us at the embassy on May 4, 2016.

Then I emailed Clayton to offer to pay for his travel and lodging so he could be there. In a series of emails he warned me about things that could go wrong at the meeting. Eventually he said he wouldn't be attending, knowing that it would cost us money and fearing that too much attention would be focused on MIA Recoveries. I was disappointed since I knew that the embassy wanted more information about MIA Recoveries; after all, they would be the ones going to China. But I decided to go ahead with the meeting.

Shiquan and his associate met us outside the huge, gated embassy of the People's Republic of China. It was impressive. We toured the embassy itself, drinking in the magnificent paintings, jade, vases, and, of course, red carpet. Eventually the four of us sat down in a cozy thirty-five-seat conference room and began our discussions.

In essence, Shiquan told us that the embassy would be willing to recommend to the minister of foreign affairs that a search for CNAC No. 60 take place. His condition was that the search take place with a civilian contractor, with or without DPAA support. This was a definite step forward, and, with MIA Recoveries in mind as the contractor, I was really pleased and excited.

The embassy required in-depth information about MIA Recoveries and Clayton Kuhles. As Shiquan pointed out, the embassy would be embarrassed if the minister asked questions they could not answer. This seemed a reasonable request.

When we left, Barb and I felt we had an open path to a recovery effort, needing only to get some information from Clayton. On May 5, I emailed Clayton a list of questions that I considered necessary to ease embassy minds. His only response was on May 9: "If Hao Chen or the PLA doesn't recover the remains by late summer, then I'll work on self-funding an archaeological investigation of the site in search of the remains. I'll be involving local Chinese personnel."

I replied the same day that I had no information that Hao Chen would be doing any work in Yunnan, only that he was planning on a return there in the summer. As I understood it, Chen was going as a part of a documentary effort and was not attempting to do any excavating. He had no partners at the moment and had some other projects he was involved in. It appeared that Chen would not be able to take part in any CNAC No. 60 effort.

Disappointingly, I heard nothing further from Clayton, so I assumed I had to try a new direction. I emailed Shiquan about MIA Recoveries and he sent back a comforting message, sympathizing with me and saying that he was making efforts to help us. He told me to take it easy and wait to see what the future would bring. His reassurances were helpful but did not have the effect I was looking for.

Many months earlier I had corresponded briefly with Mark Noah at History Flight in Marathon, Florida, whose organization had recovered a number of MIA remains in the Asia-Pacific area. I now sent him a brief summary of our situation, with a packet of information about the history of our search. I also emailed Webb, Linda, and Linnington, telling them of my meeting at the Chinese embassy and MIA Recoveries' position and asked for their thoughts. Webb wrote back immediately that he would be in touch. Then on May 20 he emailed:

Hello Bob,

Thank you for allowing me the time to speak with some of our China analysts here to get some information for you. As I mentioned to you in an earlier email, we had a delegation meet with Chinese officials in China the end of April. During that meeting the PLA Archivists they advised they were investigating Chinese Mountaineering groups in the area who might be able to access the crash site. I think you can understand they are concerned about the safety of the personnel that would attempt to get to the site. They reiterated to our delegation that they have the lead on this effort.

   I understand your urgency to get a team to the site in order to attempt to evaluate the site to determine if a recovery effort would be possible. However, in this case I think we would be best served to give the Chinese a little more time to locate a mountaineering team and if they are not successful we can offer some options. We have contact with Clayton Kuhles of MIA Recoveries and Mark Noah of History Flight and can work with them or other groups should the Chinese look to us for groups that could mount an effort to get to the site.

Respectfully,
Johnie

I emailed Shiquan with that information; he replied positively and said that the Chinese would respond to DPAA and the embassy would not make further efforts to push for a search. Everything would be between DPAA and the Ministry of Foreign Affairs or PLA. While others looked on the results of the April meeting with some optimism, I felt that it was simply another way for the Chinese to exert their dominance over the process.

In spite of Mark Noah's indication of interest in the search, he did not send the materials I had asked for as ammunition for the embassy in their request for a search, so now MIA Recoveries, History Flight, and the embassy appeared to be off the team I had hoped would move the process forward. In a sense I was back to square one, the day of discovery in 2011. It was a pretty bleak picture for Jimmie's return.

On June 8 I did get a message from Clayton giving his reason for backing away from the embassy request for information. He was concerned that any connection with the Chinese government would jeopardize his future status with DPAA. His suggestion, made previously, was that he mount a self-funded, private expedition, hire local guides in Dali, and simply enter China on a tourist visa and proceed from there. He would not seek any prior approvals from Chinese authorities, and should anyone question his presence, he would simply declare that he was on a humanitarian mission. He was certain he would find the remains, if there were any, and promised to turn them over to the embassy in Beijing or a more convenient consular office. Given Chinese attitudes toward anything of such a questionable nature, their treatment could be rather harsh, so I was not encouraging. But this left me with no alternatives and with the Chinese still in complete control.

In an email I sent to DPAA in mid-June I asked for a status report on our case. Webb's answer did little to ease my frustration. He was not overly optimistic. Things had not looked too bright before, and now Webb's tone told me that DPAA was not going to take an aggressive approach with the Chinese. That was not a happy moment.

A real feeling of betrayal came on June 21, when Clayton emailed me that DPAA director Linnington had resigned to take a job with the troubled Wounded Warrior Project. In my early communications with Linnington, he had promised that he would straighten out the confusion in the army's MIA recovery effort. He had an excellent reputation, and I believed he was capable of doing just that. His quitting left that promise unfulfilled.

I continued to try to keep things moving. I emailed Mark Noah asking if he was still interested in China, and he replied immediately that History Flight was very much interested in working in China if the Chinese approved a search. He ordered his staff to forward the materials he had used in gaining approval from the Philippine government to do recoveries in Philippine territories. The information was concise and impressive, and I felt it would answer any questions about the legitimacy of History Flight. I sent that summary to Shiquan, only to find that he would be out of the office until July 21.

I emailed Hao Chen to find out what his plans were, if any, since the summer months were disappearing. He responded that he still had plans to go to Yunnan that summer for his documentary but had no dates or specifics, so that was likely another dead end.

I emailed Webb at DPAA, pointing out that we had given China three months to find a search organization, and that we had two organizations ready to do the job, MIA Recoveries and History Flight. Even though Clayton had decided not to work with the embassy, he was willing to work with DPAA. There still seemed to be bad blood between MIA and DPAA, but Clayton felt he could work with them. I felt at that time that History Flight would be a better choice, but did not express any preference.

Webb replied the next day that he was at the VFW convention in Charlotte but would report next week. In my reply, I suggested that the VFW might help in our efforts to get Jimmie home. In 1929, in spite of the tensions that existed when the Allied Expeditionary Forces left the USSR with their tail between their legs, the VFW had managed to send an expedition into northern Russia and recover eighty-five bodies left behind.

I heard nothing from DPAA, so I emailed again the next week and, in few words, Webb again said that he was not optimistic. With that attitude from DPAA, I thought my embassy route was the best to take, forgetting DPAA. So I contacted Mark at History Flight. But he was on vacation in Vermont, so, with Shiquan in China, things were quiet for several weeks.

I contacted Shiquan on August 16 see if he needed more information. He promptly replied, asking when Mark was coming back and if Mark could give him a résumé. As soon as Mark returned from Vermont, he forwarded his résumé to me and I sent it on to the embassy on August 10. So when Shiquan asked for it again on the 16th, I was a bit puzzled, but I resent it, and Shiquan promptly acknowledged receipt.

In his request for the second résumé, Shiquan also mentioned that he was forwarding our request to Beijing, but he was very vague about just what he had asked for. I hoped that meant he had forwarded a recommendation as well, but I made no assumptions.

With the momentum slowing down, and the search for remains seeming to have an impassable hurdle in China, I began to think of other ways to acknowledge Jimmie's place in history so that future generations would know of his sacrifice and that of so many others. In China Jim's name was inscribed on the very impressive Monument to the Aviator Martyrs in Nanjing, and a new memorial plaque had been established at the Civil Aviation Museum in Beijing, thanks to the hard work and dedication of Angie Chen. But there was nothing in the U.S. to mark his passing.

Although we were still waiting for word from Beijing on Shiquan's request for permission to enter Yunnan Province, I decided to pursue a headstone for Jimmie from the Department of Veterans Affairs. While there were numerous acknowledgments of Jimmie's sacrifice in China, he had no grave, marker, or headstone anywhere in this country, and I felt he deserved some lasting marker. The VA had recently opened a new cemetery just north of us, the Cape Canaveral National Cemetery, so I decided to start there. I talked to a very nice young lady who informed me that all they could do was to put Jimmie's name on a Wall of Remembrance that was expected to be available sometime in 2017.

During the years we had been on our quest, I had met other family groups with MIA members and who were stymied by problems similar to ours. One was a group dedicated to bringing home the remains of the crew and passengers of a C-47 that crashed after the war, in March 1946. That crash was doubly tragic because, besides the eleven fatalities of crew and passengers, the plane carried the remains of forty-two Americans who had died in Japanese prison camps. Most of the passengers who were killed were members of the Graves Registration Team that had been involved in disinterring the bodies. MIA Recoveries, Inc. had reported discovering the wreckage in 2009, and word had spread to the families of both those killed in the crash and of the prisoners. The families convinced JPAC to do a preliminary search for the site and to look for the remains of those aboard, reportedly buried in a local cemetery. JPAC did send a team to the site but reported that the aircraft wreckage was not of a C-47 but an airliner built by Convair. That, of course, was devastating to the families involved.

I had read that one of the fliers who died in a Japanese prison was given a headstone in Arlington and provided a full military funeral, even though his body was never recovered. That gave me a new direction to pursue, but I first took another tack and applied for any medals to which Jim might be entitled. I thought he should receive at least a Purple Heart. As previously mentioned, CNAC and other Pan Am pilots had been granted veteran status under Public Law 95-202 in 1992, and some CNAC pilots had been awarded a Distinguished Flying Cross or an Air Medal; I reasoned that if I could get awards for Jim, citing these decorations might help in getting him U.S. burial rights.

I decided to ask my congressman, Bill Posey, for his help. His response came on September 6 when he enclosed a letter from the Department of the Army stating that Jim was not eligible for a Purple Heart or an Air Medal because he was not engaged in combat with a hostile force.

Actually, we don't know if he was engaged with the Japanese or not, since the Japanese had a fighter base less than three hundred miles from his crash site. In any event, I asked friends at CNAC about decorations, and they said that Distinguished Flying Crosses had been awarded to fifteen CNAC pilots in 1996, so I asked Congressman Posey to find out why Jim would not be entitled to a DFC. His response was to forward a letter from the air force outlining the paperwork required for awards of decorations from World War II: an eyewitness account of the death or wounding and a full explanation of the circumstances of the event, both of which were patently impossible. No one witnessed the crash—it had not even been discovered until sixty-nine years later—and only one CNAC member still survived who was flying in 1942, Moon Chin, who was ninety-nine. I asked Posey's military specialist if he could intervene on our behalf, but he said that if the congressman pursued the matter any further, "he would lose all credibility." End of his assistance.

# 22

## Disappointment

Tripp Alyn at the AVG Flying Tiger Association asked if I was interested in attending the Atlanta AVG reunion on September 21 to 25, 2016. He suggested I could have my photo taken at the Hunter Robbins Flight Museum with John Dean's original portrait, then participate in a panel discussion at the Warbird Air Show on September 24.

Tripp said I could meet with Ken Tilley, an army historian at Fort Rucker, Alabama, who had retired from DPAA and whom Tripp believed had some inside information on our search efforts. Tilley had told Tripp that he had been issued a gag order that prevented him from contacting me, so I was pretty eager to have a conversation with him. Aside from Tilley, the panel would include Hao Chen, my former contact from the CNAC 2015 reunion, but Tilley did not show up until after I had left and the reunion was ending.

I had a very interesting few days at the reunion, getting a glimpse into the interests of the next generation of AVG members. Two AVG original members were there, and Frank Losonsky, a P-40 mechanic, who got to go up in a P-40 at the ripe old age of ninety-six. But my meeting with Tilley never happened, which was a definite disappointment.

When I got home I had an email from Shiquan; he had heard from Beijing on his suggestion for a CNAC No. 60 search, and they would give him a formal reply by mid-October. So at least we had some hope that something would happen in the next few weeks. In the same batch of emails was a message from Johnie Webb, saying that a crew had just returned from China and discussions with the PLA. They had an update on our case, but Webb thought it best to give me the results by phone rather than email.

To further complicate life, Tripp called from Pensacola explaining that Tilley had been attending a funeral in Alabama, which explained why he was not in Atlanta. Tripp cautioned me that Tilley said I had few friends at DPAA. I could not fathom why. I knew Clayton had been in disfavor, but apparently that had carried over to me.

Some time passed before I heard from Tilley on November 7, in an email referring to the fact that when he was still at DPAA, he had been served with a gag order, requiring him to cease any contact with families of the missing. Since he had been one source of information in the past, that shut off much of the accurate picture of events. In his email he said, "The only reason I got involved was to keep families informed with the truth and not keep leading them as had been done for years." Startling news to say the least, but not totally shocking, for we had had suspicions over the years.

Tilley became even more specific in an email on November 8, 2016:

> My initial intent was to get as much medical information/descriptions as possible as to help identify the remains. I contacted families of all three [Burma AVG Recoveries], thinking it was part of my job as an investigator. When word got out, my leadership at DPAA came to me and told me that I wasn't supposed to contact families as I might "mislead them" or give them "false hope." When I defended myself and told them I needed all information I could get, including from families, they said it was not my job. Ironically on a trip to India, my general and I had some time together and I told him what I had done and his comment was, "Why wouldn't you contact a family for information to help close a case?" The lab and Johnie Webb did not like his answers and felt that they knew the best policy.
>
> Because the three AVG Burma cases involved getting DNA and contacting DPAA and their Congressional representatives, those had to be looked at closely. The lab resented this and absolutely shut down any

cooperation with me on the case[s]. The person I originally worked with in the lab (now gone) had a gag order put on her to not work with me and we had no further contact.

He said that he could see in my emails my frustration at not getting answers. He finally could not take it anymore and emailed me the true state of affairs. It wasn't much of a revelation, but it was enough to enrage Webb, who exploded and went to Tilley's boss (a navy commander), who ordered Tilley to "not contact any family about any case." Tilley's explanation that we were being misled or lied to by Webb did not matter. "At that point I kept reading your emails but could not answer."

Tilley left DPAA in December 2015. He told me, "All who know me know that I ALWAYS tell the truth and feel that is the best way DPAA can work with families. Too many have been misled, told half-truths or outright lied to through the years and I refused to do that. The way things were done eventually drove me away from DPAA [to] pursue my career as an Army historian."

I asked him if he could provide some specifics about the hostility between Clayton Kuhles and DPAA, and before that, JPAC. Tilley was very candid in pointing out some of the agency's concerns about Clayton. It boiled down to a conflict between JPAC and Clayton regarding C-47 No. 8308, which MIA Recoveries had found near Birmani Kami, India, in 2009. JPAC sent a team, according to Tilley, prematurely, and they found discrepancies between their findings and Clayton's. Even the *Stars and Stripes*, the military's own newspaper, believed the JPAC mission was poorly conceived and organized. The paper reported, "The site was never properly vetted by the JPAC excavation decision board, and was fast-tracked based on questionable assumptions and procedural missteps." Subsequently JPAC said it was not a C-47 but a Convair from a Pakistani airline that crashed in 1953. The paper also reported that the cost of the failed mission was $502,000.[1]

Another strange fact emerged involving remains from that crash. MIA Recoveries had reported that a gravesite had been established near the wreckage, which contained not only the passengers and crew but the remains of POWs who had died in captivity and been buried in the Rangoon area. But JPAC's expedition mentioned nothing about the grave, yet Clayton maintained that services for the dead were conducted regularly by locals. In his report to JPAC, Clayton wrote:

> The villagers recounted seeing many bodies scattered about. The villagers collected all the human remains they could find and brought those remains down to their village. The remains were then buried in an impromptu cemetery on the edge of the village. A large metal cross fashioned from the aircraft wreckage was erected within the cemetery plot. The villagers said the large metal cross stood in the cemetery for many years, and disappeared about 5–10 years ago after an especially heavy rainstorm. They think an earthen embankment collapsed and allowed the cross to fall into the nearby creek where it probably washed downstream.[2]

It is difficult to imagine that a search by JPAC could fail to turn up the designated burial site of forty-two POW remains and eleven crew members, but that seemed to be the case.

Adding to that dispute was the fact that the families involved tried to contact MIA Recoveries but were never able to establish any communications. So their original joy at the discovery completely disappeared. However, they were successful in getting Lt. John Kelly a headstone and full military honors in Arlington, even though his remains are still in India. Kelly was one of the prisoners who survived a B-24 shoot-down but died of his injuries in the Rangoon prison due to lack of medical attention from the Japanese.

To add to this confusion, I need to add some of my conclusions. I had briefly investigated Indian aircraft crashes and learned that there had been two Convair crashes in postwar India, one near New Delhi in 1967 and another in 1953 on the border of East Pakistan and India. I believed that meant the crash was close to Pakistan, many miles from the reported crash site visited by JPAC. However, when my daughter, who spent a year in Pakistan and is married to a Pakistani, read this manuscript, told me East Pakistan is now Bangladesh. So I reviewed my hastily gathered data and went to another website, Pacific Wrecks, which held extensive information:

The aircraft was one of three Convair CV 240s sold to Pakistani Orient Airways in 1949. On March 14, 1953 it departed Karachi headed for Bangladesh's Dhaka Airport with sixteen passengers and crew aboard. The pilot attempted to descend in bad weather and crashed into a mountain south of Kalahasahar. All aboard were killed and buried in a mass grave near the crash site.

WRECKAGE

This aircraft crashed into the Longthrai Regional Forest in Dhalai District, State of Tripura in India. The crash site is located between two hillocks (Kala Tilla) near Chandrahansapara. During the monsoon season, the area floods causing wreckage to wash downstream.

During 1955, the wife of the pilot attempted to visit the crash site with the help of local people and riding an elephant. At the wreckage, she held a religious service.

During 2003, Ms. Parrott (daughter of passenger Kenneth Alex Parrott) traveled to the region and attempted to visit the crash site but was unable due to threats in the area.

On November 5, 2009 this crash site was visited by Clayton Kuhles / MIA Recoveries. He incorrectly identified the wreckage as associated with C-47B Dakota 43-48308. He photographed a propeller assembly and posted a single photograph that shows a panel with black stenciled "141-24/25569" but no other photos of this stencil for other angles or wider views.

During November 2013, the same crash site Clayton Kuhles / MIA Recoveries visited was investigated by both an investigation team (IT) and recovery team (RT) from Joint POW/MIA Accounting Command (JPAC) and coded the site IN-00264. The team positively identified the crash site as a Convair CV-240 based on the engine crankshaft associated with a Pratt & Whitney R-2800 engine and an inspection stamp with "CVSD," the designation for Consolidated/Vultee. Both of these points of identification prove this crash site is associated with a Convair CV-240 registration AP-AEG, not a Douglas C-47 or DC-3.

MEMORIALS

After the crash, a memorial was built for Kenneth Alex Parrott at the Border Security Force (BSF) Camp in Nalkata, Tripura, India. The memorial has a concrete base with a metal cross with a plaque at each side. The plaques are in both English and Bengali and read: "Kenneth Alec Parrott Born 4 March 1921 Tragically died here on 13 March 1953. Husband to RoseMary Father to Jeffery and Beverley. We have loved you and missed you all our lives." During 2005 the Parrott family provided funding to establish and fund the Kenneth Parrott Nursery School at Tripura.

RELATIVES
Beverley Parrott (daughter of Kenneth Alex Parrott)[3]

I believe the flight path and crash site location are the reason for the confusion with the C-47 on the part of JPAC and MIA Recoveries. But is it possible both aircraft crashed in the same location and the wreckage is intermingled? It is DPAA's contention that the C-47 tragically went down in the Indian Ocean off the coast of India on its way from Rangoon to Calcutta and will never be found. But both references verify that a grave exists containing the remains of the sixteen Convair victims and/or the fifty-three Americans. When I questioned Clayton about the discrepancies, he maintained that JPAC went to a different site than the one he reported, which turned out to be where the Convair crashed. The area is dense jungle and very hilly, so it is possible that there were two separate crashes, first the C-47 in 1946 and then the Convair in 1953.

To add another dimension to the mystery, the *Telegraph*, a Calcutta newspaper, ran an article in its Sunday edition of January 15, 2012, in which it says:

> Throwing light on some events related to the crash, police sources said an American passenger David Campbell had succumbed to his injuries a few days after the crash. His younger brother Tony Campbell, who came to know of the crash and his brother's death from army records and the internet, had come to Tripura in the mid-nineties when insurgency was at its height in the state.
>
> "He wanted to visit the spot but was prevented from doing so by the police on the ground that the place was a hotbed of militancy and he might be kidnapped or killed," a senior police officer said.[4]

Another news item states that on January 14, 2012, a team of searchers from the 34th Assam Rifles also found an aircraft crash site, which they identified as the C-47 that went down in May 1946, the same aircraft reported by Clayton.[5] So there is a strong possibility that two separate wreck sites were visited, one by MIA Recoveries, and one by JPAC. Even *Stars and Stripes* claims the two searches were seven miles apart. The report from JPAC did not include the exact location of their search, so it is possible the two searchers were examining different wreckage, and there has been no follow-up by DPAA on the grave locations.

I was anxious to hear the results of the long-awaited October 26 meeting of DPAA, the Chinese Ministry of Foreign Affairs, and the PLA. Webb had promised that he would set up a conference call after the team returned, which would include those who had been at the meeting. I emailed him on November 1, and he assured me he would be in touch as soon as the team members had consolidated their notes. I was not expecting much, since everyone had been so negative, but I wanted to know what steps we might take if everything indicated we would never get Chinese permission to search. Finally, he sent a summary of the meeting with the unhappy news. But the real blow was the following email of November 10, 2016:

> Per the Chinese, members of the PLA-A (Archives) and mountaineers assembled in Dali, Yunnan earlier in the month and were prepared to attempt ascent to the site to take photos and video for the family. A Chinese source close to Mr. Willett, Mr. Chen, was also present in Dali. He advised that Mr. Willett was satisfied with the photographs previously received from the site (3rd Party source, Mr. Clayton Kuhles, 2011) and required no additional photos or video. Per Mr. Chen, Mr. Willett's request was for remains only. The Chinese believe there is no possibility of recovering remains at this site and therefore, determined that the dangerous ascent was unnecessary since the family was satisfied with the 2011 photographs.

That really staggered me. I was ready to find Hao Chen and read him the riot act, but he was not available. I emailed him of my disappointment and informed him that he could not, and was not to, represent my thoughts in any actions with Chinese.

On November 15 he sent me this email: "I said what? I made no statement to anyone, Chinese or American whatsoever regarding this matter. I am thoroughly puzzled. I do not know why anyone would represent me in this matter, but I will be glad to help clear up any confusion. Let me know how I can help." If the Mr. Chen at the meeting in Dali was not Hao Chen, then who was he? And why was he speaking for me?

I forwarded Hao's message to Webb and requested to speak with a member of the team that attended the meeting. He replied on Saturday, November 19, that he would have a call to me with a team member on Monday. Monday came and went, but on Tuesday an email said he needed to have a member of the team who had attended the meeting on the call, but she was not available. Then an automated call said he and his fellow conferee would be on leave until the 28th.

I had emailed Linda McFadyen earlier asking if she could set up a meeting with DPAA officials on a planned Washington Thanksgiving visit, but I had had no response, so I emailed again on November 22. Her response to that was that she too would be on leave until the 28th. I was not terribly surprised that everyone was gone, since it was Thanksgiving. But since I was going to be in Washington from November 24 to 28, I thought I might get to see someone.

Finally, on the 29th, my last day in Washington, Linda emailed that two DPAA members were available and could see me that afternoon. My daughter took me to the DPAA office in Arlington, where I met with Robert Goeke and Lt. Cmdr. Dan Colon.

It was a really interesting meeting, giving me a new slant. Colon had actually been at the China meeting; he said the Ministry of Foreign Affairs and the PLA were both dedicated to an examination of the site, but the wreck being at 13,200 feet posed enormous risk to any team sent, and that was their concern. He said that DPAA was still committed to bringing up the mission in future meetings. Goeke was more pessimistic, agreeing that safety was a genuine concern. We discussed many other aspects of the case, including the fact that no one had been to the site to record the actual conditions.

Goeke later suggested that drones could examine the site and offer some information on the potential for the search effort. I did some investigating and found a drone company in Australia that had recently done work in Yunnan Province in China. They reported no problems in going as high as fifteen thousand feet, but pointed out the effects of temperature and winds, which are definitely a factor in the Cangshan area. I reported this to Colon, who thought it might be useful for their technology people.

Back on track with the DPAA, I finally got an email from Linda that a conference call would take place December 8 or 9 to answer my concerns about the DPAA report on the October meeting. But both dates passed without any word, another disappointment. I emailed Goeke and Colon that the agency had lost all credibility for me.

Finally, after a number of emails setting dates and times, the phone rang and Webb and a woman named Gwen from DPAA who had attended the October meeting were on the other end. The conversation went pretty directly to the October meeting. I asked Gwen about the introduction of Mr. Chen's remarks, and she gave me the same line as Webb had emailed, that the Chinese had accepted that input and had backed off any attempts to investigate further. I asked specifically if this meant that we were at a dead end, and both agreed that this development spelled the end.

At that point I was really upset and suggested that maybe DPAA had not put forth their best effort. Gwen shot back that they weren't totally sure that the site really contained CNAC No. 60. That was another indication to me that they were looking for outs. When I asked her what it would take for them to be certain, she said only that there was an element of doubt. After five years of setting dates and negotiations with the Chinese to go to the site, they weren't even sure it was the right aircraft? Ridiculous!

It went downhill from that point. I brought up the matter of Mr. Chen and said that if this mystery man's remark was the only reason to cancel the site inspection, I wanted DPAA to go back to the Chinese and tell them the Willett family is not satisfied with the existing five-year-old photos, and that we denied any connection with Chen. They acknowledged that it was a valid point and said they would get back to the PLA with my rather strong views.

It seemed very clear that DPAA would not be pressing the Chinese on examining the site, and if they did, they would back off at the earliest possible time, using the same reasoning as the Chinese: the safety of the search team. It did seem odd to me that a nation with the human rights history that China had established would be that concerned about the risks taken by experienced mountaineers, using all the modern safety measures. I knew that safety was not the real reason, but the politics of our two countries. Whether it was danger, local reluctance, or something else, there seemed to be no interest in a search for the remains of James S. Browne, John J. Dean, or K. L. Yang. True to my suspicions, DPAA has never raised the issue of Mr. Chen with the Chinese.

Only a few days later came an email from Shiquan that closed the door on any help he could give. He began by saying that when he was a "freshman" and had been in the U.S. only a few months, he thought he could help get Jim's remains back and give his family peace after so long a period of not knowing what had happened to him. He was encouraged in May 2014 when the PLA transferred Jim's records to the U.S. Everything seemed so promising, but his term in the U.S. was ending and he would be returning to China in June. He said no real progress had been made and there seemed to be no hope of further success in the near future. That effectively slammed the door to the embassy that had once been wide open.

With those developments, my thoughts drifted to the many efforts to bring Jim home. Why had the Flying Tigers had so little interest in Dean when they had pursued other MIAs with good results? Had Gwen denied the positive identification of CNAC No. 60 because it was Clayton who discovered our C-47? If Ken Tilley's comments were true, why were we families being lied to and being denied access to information? Was there something about CNAC No. 60 that was being covered up? Why, when the Ministry of Foreign Affairs left the door open for civilian mountaineers to do the search, were the two U.S. organizations who were qualified never contacted or considered? Who was this mysterious Mr. Chen who carried such weight at the October 26 meeting? Looking back, I now realized that the Chinese had used other excuses to avoid the crash site: the seventieth-anniversary celebration, then local officials, and finally safety. And all this as the awarding of military decorations from our own government had been quashed by the need for paperwork.

One other nagging question was why so much hostility was aimed at Clayton Kuhles. He was probably the most knowledgeable individual in the country on the subject of downed aircraft in the China-Burma-India theater. The depth of the DPAA's distrust of Clayton was evident when Ken Tilley revealed, "No investigators will work with him. They don't trust him."

As I pieced it together, the distrust stemmed from the downed C-47 Clayton found in Tripura Prefecture, India. He reported it and alerted the families of the crew, and they were successful in convincing JPAC to do a preliminary search. When the second search determined that it was the wreckage of a Convair probably was from a Pakistani airline, and that the piece of aluminum with the construction number on it could not be found, that led DPAA to the conclusion that Kuhles had fabricated the number. It may not have occurred to them that if Clayton left the piece of aluminum out in the open when he left, a local villager could have made a dozen soup bowls out of it. And I questioned why JPAC did not investigate the cemetery Clayton mentioned so specifically in his JPAC report. The cemetery was less than two miles from the wreckage and should have been the focal point of any search. All very strange, with so many questions remaining. I believe that either DPAA or the Chinese have knowledge they are not sharing, for reasons known only to themselves.

Whatever the truth is, that disagreement and other more minor concerns of DPAA, which caused the souring of MIA Recoveries and DPAA relations, may have been justified, but it has undoubtedly hurt the chances of investigations of some of Clayton's finds, including ours. The expertise he has could certainly be of use to MIA recoveries in China-Burma-India locations. And there does seem to be some credibility to Clayton's argument that the investigations of C-47 8308 were at different locations. However, DPAA is rather adamant that MIA Recoveries is not to be used.

In the beginning of 2017, a flurry of emails went back and forth and brought a breath of hope for a time, but that too was extinguished. I had emailed DPAA and copied the Chinese embassy about a Flying Tiger Museum in Guilin that would be having a ceremony in March. It was celebrating the arrival of a C-47, *Buzz Buggy*, that had been flown all the way from Australia and, in a commemoration flight, across the Hump. That 5,600-mile journey merits its own book, the crew having survived two blown engines. It was to have taken eight days but ended up taking three months and an inordinate amount of cash. The C-47 finally did arrive in Guilin and was donated by the Flying Tiger Historical Organization to the Flying Tiger Heritage Park in Guilin. My thought was that this was an appropriate time to announce that an excavation of the CNAC No. 60 wreck site was approved and would take place shortly. Since the three dead airmen were Flying Tigers in the Chinese version of the term, an effort to recover their remains would fit emotionally into the theme of Guilin Park, a testimony to the American young men lost in the War against Japanese Aggression. To no one's surprise, I received no answer to my suggestion.

One of my final email exchanges started in December 2016, when I emailed Shiquan that all avenues to success seemed to be closed and that I was "resting my case." In January I got an email from him explaining that it was the local officials in Yunnan Province who were objecting to the excavation and that the Ministry of Foreign Affairs could not overrule the objections of the locals. When I showed the email to Rob Goeke at DPAA he fired right back, suggesting we could take a different approach from the one we had used on the Ministry. He asked me to find out what the locals objected to, which might give us a lead. But Shiquan's response was that it was because of dangerous conditions, the same objection others had used.

Then I thought that I would go to China and meet with Yunnan officials so they could see the family's interest and possibly change their minds. With that in mind, I again emailed Shiquan, who had earlier offered to help if I wanted to visit China. I told him I was considering a short visit and asked him to help arrange meetings with officials there. Instead he scolded me, reminding me that I had said I was "resting my case," and that a meeting with officials might prove awkward. That quashed any ideas of my returning to China.

I made a last effort to get help by visiting Congressman Bill Posey. I had no appointment when Donna and I walked into his Brevard County office in Viera, Florida, but Rob Medina, the congressman's community relations and military liaison officer, was available and willing to spend some time with us. I was primarily interested in getting help finding information on awards for which Jimmie had been eligible.

On a number of occasions Posey's office had corresponded with authorities in the air force and the army on the search effort and possible decorations. To my knowledge, he had sent several letters to the services but had received negative responses, indicating that Jim was not entitled to awards unless paperwork could be provided from his unit commander, who could verify his death and provide an eyewitness to the event. After one negative reply from the air force, I sent copies of the Defense Department's summary of Jim's service and his death. That apparently was not sufficient.

We also discussed the search possibilities, and Medina brought out copies of the DPAA responses saying that the Chinese felt the search was too dangerous. When I brought up the subject of Mr. Chen's interference at the October meeting, he said that the DPAA still maintained the only reason they would not do a search was because of the danger. I later sent him a copy of the email from DPAA stating that a search party had been formed and was ready to go, until Mr. Chen said that Mr. Willett was satisfied with the photos taken by MIA Recoveries and so no visit to bring back photo evidence of the wreck was necessary. With that, the congressman's interest in Jimmie Browne and Robert L. Willett ceased.

# 23

## Square of the Chivalrous Friends of China

Just when it seemed as if there was no progress in any direction and no strong push for further efforts, on July 11, 2018, I received an email from Angie Chen, in Guangzhou, giving me some really startling news. Angie had been a constant champion of CNAC in both China and the U.S., taking every opportunity to push for developments that would enhance the public's view of CNAC's role in World War II and aviation overall. Her first item of good news was political: one of the stumbling blocks to our search approval, the Yunnan minister of foreign affairs, had retired. And Angie had heard from another longtime CNAC booster in China, Ge Shuya, that other government officials wanted to open a dialogue about the search. Ge was planning to attend meetings a few days later to see if he could get a feeling for what was ahead.

In another surprising bit of news, Angie announced that a group of Second Generation CNAC members in China had visited the Jianchuan Museum in Sichuan Province. Second Generation CNAC is a different organization from the U.S. CNAC Association, made up of Chinese descendants of China National Aviation Corporation staff members. They were interested in maintaining a presence of the old, pioneer airline. In their visit to the Jianchuan Museum they had discovered an area called the Square of the Chivalrous Friends of China. In this area were forty sculptured busts of foreigners who had aided China during the fight against the Japanese invaders.

And to my great surprise, there was a bust of "James Brown"! It was my cousin Jimmie, with his smiling face taken right from the Riverside 1940 *Bayonet*, memorialized in southwestern China.

Angie provided me with charts and descriptions of the area where Jimmie had his place. The Jianchuan Museum is a cluster of fifteen museums, and the Square of the Chivalrous Friends of China is in the one devoted to the Japanese invasion and World War II. The forty busts were done in 2016, and so are a recent addition to the honors paid to Allied friends of China. The figures represent ten countries; the U.S. has the most, at fourteen, and Russia is next with seven. Three American busts are AVG pilots led by General Chennault, two are journalists, and other honorees are doctors, missionaries, and others who risked their lives to protect Chinese families. Jimmie is the only CNAC representative.

From the minute I heard about Jim's place in the Chinese museum, I knew I had to see it and began planning almost immediately. Son Tom came into the picture once again, and I started pricing tickets. In my delicate physical condition, I decided to blow the savings and go business class for both of us. Due to schedule constraints and some previous travel commitments, we decided on October 10 to 16, 2018.

During the months before our departure Angie was doing her best to arrange meetings with various government bodies as well as a civilian foundation. As the trip drew closer, she grew less optimistic about our meeting with the minister of foreign affairs in Yunnan, so we decided not to include Kunming. However, Ge Shuya had contacted a Dali group called Shenzhen Longyue Charity Foundation, a nationwide charitable organization dedicated to victims of war, who expressed interest in a Dali memorial. So we included Dali in our short China visit. Angie had decided she wanted to be our guide, translator, and planner, so our email correspondence grew by the day. A positive turn of events occurred when the Foundation announced that they would send a representative to Chengdu instead of our having to get to Dali, so we scrubbed the Dali stop.

On October 10 we left home and overnighted in Los Angeles, boarding our China Eastern flight at 1:50 p.m. on the 11th. Business class was nice, but we found that we would be stopping in Nanjing and going through immigration there, which made the total flight time longer. I still am not sure how many hours were involved in the transpacific travel, but even with the lie-flat seat in business, it was a long trip.

True to her word, even though it was close to midnight, Angie greeted us at the Chengdu airport with a driver. Somehow the hour-long limo ride to the Four Points Sheraton Hotel in Anren seemed much longer. We checked in and promptly went to bed, planning to meet Angie about noon the next day, the 12th, to be driven to the museum.

A group of about thirty members of the Second Generation CNAC had gathered amid the busts in the Square of the Chivalrous Friends of China. The museum's founder and director, Fan Jianchuan, was unable to attend, but the assistant director started the formalities, praising the wartime allies, particularly America. I said a word of thanks for our hosts, giving great credit to the addition of Jimmie's bust and how much it meant to all of us. Then Tom placed a bouquet of beautiful yellow flowers at the foot of Jim's bust, and I placed mine, followed by each spectator placing a single yellow bloom with the others. The brief service closed with one minute of silence and three ceremonial nods in unison. It was a great moment.

The square is open and the busts are spaced eight across in a semicircle, five rows deep. It is impressive and somber, and except for Jimmie, the visages of the past are unsmiling and serious. Jimmie's smile seemed to lessen the sadness of the square and gave a little relief to the stoic faces of the others. Most of the busts were gray and dark, but three, for unknown reasons, were sculpted in bright gold and gleamed in the morning sun. The entrance to the walled courtyard was guarded by two stone soldiers grimly aware of their responsibilities.

Afterward we mingled with the Second Generation members, and, although no one spoke English, gestures and smiles showed their respect and their thanks, and I hope mine to them. We were able to wander around the compound and spent much time in the museum that housed the collections of items received from Americans who were involved in the war. The walls of that display hall featured photos of all AVG members, from floor to ceiling. John Dean's photo was one of the several hundred. There were pieces of an ATC C-187 that had crashed in Tibet and that the museum had recovered, displayed in a frosty-looking diorama. Other items were more plebian: broken shovels by the score, piles of canteens and helmets, plus settings for photographs of units that were part of the China-Burma-India scene. It was a wonderful tribute to America and its role in China's history.

As we wandered the pathways of the cluster of buildings, we found time to stop for a tea break and a little more interaction with the Second Generation members. Angie, our faithful translator, explained that this group was from Beijing, although there were others from different parts of the country. Their parents or relatives were all copilots, radiomen, or mechanics or played other roles in the early and wartime days of China's aviation.

As we sat having our Chinese tea, Angie's phone rang and she was told that Fan Jianchuan, the Big Man himself, was in his office waiting for us, so we hastened to gather the group together. His office was large and very rustic—no secretarial entrance foyer, it was open and decorated with a variety of photos and trophies. Fan is a very attractive, midfifties, casual executive who puts everyone at ease, despite the language barrier. He seemed interested in our endeavors to bring Jimmie home, and mentioned only briefly the current squabbles between our two governments.

He did add that one of his goals in creating the museum was to illustrate to Chinese people the part America played in the war. In the Chinese school system for years there was little mention of any outside aid for China, but recently there had been renewed acknowledgment of America's help. That was made most obvious in 2015 with the celebration of the seventieth anniversary of the end of World War II, but it continued with help from people like Fan. We appreciated his spending time with us and his kindness in creating and displaying Jimmie's bust.

The next day, October 14, we were to meet with the representative from the Dali group and talk about a memorial of some kind to be erected on Cangshan Mountain. I had drawn a simple plaque stating the facts about the crash and listing the names of the crew members with a brief sentence about their sacrifice for China and the world. I was going to give it to the Dali representative as a beginning.

We met Sun Chunlong in the Sheraton coffee shop at about 9:00 a.m. on that Sunday, and at first he and Angie conversed in Chinese at some length. Eventually Angie turned to us to tell us what he had said about his organization. Their full name was Shenzhen Longyue Charity Foundation, and their mission was to help those affected by war. That included constructing memorials to the fallen, helping refugees, assisting Chinese war veterans in need, searching for Chinese MIAs throughout Asia, and generally trying to aid those who had suffered in the wars fought by China over the years. They had recovered MIAs in several nations, so he felt they had a wealth of experience in that area. The organization had been started on November 11, 2011, almost the same time that Clayton had discovered CNAC No. 60, and marked the ninety-third anniversary of the end of World War I. Although they had recovered some MIAs, they still had 823 leads to work on.

Gradually I began to understand that this meeting might lead to more than a simple memorial. After about two hours of being questioned about our case, Sun asked if we would authorize the Shenzhen Longyue Charity Foundation to undertake an excavation of CNAC No. 60. He explained they would proceed to the site, after interviewing the villagers and the PLA. They would then ascend to the site and excavate for remains. Those remains would be sent to their lab in Shanghai for identification. And all this would be funded by their organization. It was their hope to get proper clearances so they could start immediately.

I was stunned, absolutely speechless, and pretty emotional. So it was a minute or so before I could tell him how priceless his offer was. After so many years of sometimes callous and uncaring rejection of our limited efforts, we now had not only a friend but a partner. An experienced, well-funded, local, Chinese-speaking partner. I readily agreed to let the foundation take over the search and the rest of the project. We had never even considered the possibility of that kind of help coming out of our trip.

Sun had to catch a plane back to Kunming in the early afternoon. All he wanted from us was a letter from the family authorizing the foundation to proceed with the search. We fumbled around for a while as we sought to write something satisfactory, but finally Angie said she would be in Kunming on Monday and would bring him a more polished letter than the quick draft we came up with. She would give him some background material as well. Fortunately I had brought one of my packaged summaries of the flight, the crew, and the JPAC report from Clayton. I also hoped that we could keep Clayton in the project and so advised Sun. About that point I made a confession that I had refrained from mentioning anywhere in our search process: I had been part of the American forces that fought the Chinese and North Koreans in 1951. I thought that might be a problem for them, but they actually broke out in laughter at the irony of it all.

That afternoon we went back to the Jianchuan Museum, paying closer attention to the displays of American involvement. One exhibit was made up of handprints, all in red, mounted on clear glass panels; they included the prints of CNAC pilots Moon Chin and Pete Goutiere.

## Conclusion

For me, the hunt is over. I have in a sense passed to the Shenzhen Longyue Charity Foundation the fate of all our efforts. I do so with the understanding that the results they obtain will end any further searching. I have great confidence that their experience and dedication will bring every needed ingredient to establish the presence of remains at the site of the crash of CNAC No. 60. Should they find no evidence of the crew there, that too will bring finality to the quest.

There still lingers the puzzle that is China. We saw on each of our trips there that the Chinese people and their government recognize America's help during World War II. This was evident on our first trip, in 2015, at the huge luncheon we attended in Beijing after the parade, to which representatives from a number of Allied nations had been invited. Evident then too was China's compassion for our cause, when they made sure we could visit both Dali and the Nanjing Monument.

The existence of various memorials around China also pay tribute to the fallen from many nations. There is the Monument to the Aviator Martyrs in the War of Resistance against Japanese Aggression, begun many years before America's entrance in the war, and the recent museum addition. There is the plaque in the Civil Aviation Museum in Beijing that lists all the CNAC fatalities, including Jimmie and John Dean, and a display of the history of the airline and its dramatic demise. In Kunming there is a monument dedicated to the Hump pilots and crews who lost their lives during the war, and the many acknowledgments of America's role in the Jianchuan Museum near Chengdu. So there is no shortage of reminders of the contributions Americans and other foreigners made.

At the same time, there is a lack of humanitarian empathy for the families of those lost fighting for China. We saw this with the results of DPAA meetings with the Chinese when we were refused permission to excavate for remains. Given China's poor human rights history, the reason for the refusal—that the work would be too dangerous—was not convincing.

My efforts turned to establishing some sort of grave site for Jim. I considered applying for a marker in one of the national cemeteries, in Arlington National Cemetery, and in the cemetery where Jim's parents are buried. While China has its several memorials with Jim's name included, in the U.S. there is no monument or marker to acknowledge his life and death.

As that process continued, I thought about the Defense POW/ MIA Accounting Agency and its mission: to "provide the fullest possible accounting for our missing personnel to their families and the nation." The title of the agency charged with the MIA situation clearly describes its function. The key word is "accounting." It is not designed to find the missing, but simply to account for them in some way. There are still many, many sites reported to DPAA that have not been visited. There are a host of reasons for this, but there seems to be no burning desire to step up the progress. Accounting for the missing falls far short of an effort to find them and bring them home. Americans trust that our government will expend its vast resources to find those who were lost fighting the nation's battles and bring them honorably home. But that trust is misplaced.

I applaud the men and women at DPAA who venture forth to examine reported sites, sometimes encountering danger and less than luxurious surroundings. I know that their efforts are restricted by budgets over which they have little control and that it is Congress and the army that set the pace of activity. Yet one of the primary missions of DPAA is communications, and in our experience they fail badly in that responsibility. That is an unnecessary failure that borders on the criminal.

President Obama set a goal of identifying two hundred MIAs per year, yet even that minimal goal has never been met. And with eighty-three thousand MIAs, finding two hundred a year just illustrates our lack of interest in accomplishing anything significant. With all the fatalities that took place on the Hump, to my knowledge our government has returned only one U.S. airman, Pfc Mervyn E. Sims, whose remains were removed from his aircraft wreckage and taken to the U.S. consulate in India, not by JPAC but by Clayton Kuhles, and from there were finally returned to his Illinois hometown.[1] Other than that one case, our government has failed to get authorizations to remove remains from crashes in other countries, mainly India and China.

I propose that the task of locating and recovering MIAs be removed from the army, known for its impenetrable bureaucracy and inefficiency, and assigned to a civilian agency developed for that sole purpose. Aside from introducing efficiency into the process, this would remove the roadblock that the very label "U.S. Army" has proven to be when dealing with foreign governments. And we can hope that a new agency will develop a Mission Statement that has some direction to it, that is more than a series of elegant but useless phrases.

An example of such an organization is the Shenzhen Longyue Charitable Foundation, a civilian nonprofit organization whose motto is "Fulfilling Our Duty." Here are their goals:

1. Caring for the veterans of the War of Resistance against Japan.

2. Offering humanitarian aid to refugees in war zones.

3. Seeking those missing in action.

4. Comforting those who have lost loved ones.

5. Building memorial walls for our fallen soldiers.

6. Bringing home the souls of heroes of the Anti-Japanese War of Resistance.[2]

These are not vague statements but action items that are being actively pursued. Impressively, the group has so far recovered hundreds of Chinese MIAs from the mountains and fields of Burma.

It is time Americans face the realities of the MIA situation and set our course in a way that is realistic yet meaningful, and that we find those with true compassion in their hearts to lead us.

# Epilogue

You can't beat remains, kid. They'll tell the story every time.

Those words are from Daniel Ford's novel, *Remains*, a fictional story of the Flying Tigers and the tragedy of two young fliers. Their fate is finally exposed when the skeleton of one of them is discovered still strapped to his downed P-40. Without remains, no story can be complete, no ending satisfying.[1]

Our hunt may be over, but we will continue to press for organizations and individuals who may be of help in other searches, and we will push for more focus on finding and recovering MIAs. New wars may make the category of MIA a thing of the past, given technology and communications developments, but the MIAs of our past wars should not be ignored and forgotten.

Shiquan Wang has returned to China. Clayton Kuhles stands ready to tackle any MIA project. Johnie Webb at DPAA survived the JPAC episode and seems to be the main figure in our failures. And DPAA still talks about meeting with the Chinese. What purpose any such meeting would have is questionable but probably allows for the fact that a meeting, however fruitless in the past, is better than no meeting. The Shenzhen Longyue Charity Foundation still has plans to excavate the site, but dates are not yet confirmed.

And I repeat: my hunt is over.

Lest We Forget

# Notes

### 1. James Sallee "Jimmie" Browne

1. County Court of Cook County, Illinois, Consent to Adoption, dated June 8, 1921.

2. Jack Stark, "Wings for Flying Cadets," *Miami Herald*, March 3, 1940.

3. Letter from Helen Cole to author, dated March 1, 2009.

### 2. Air Transport Auxiliary

1. British Overseas Airways Corporation and James Sallee Browne, "Agreement for Service as Pilot," May 22, 1941, Montreal, ATA Archives, London.

2. Ferry Records, ATA Archives, London, undated.

3. "British Air Transport Auxiliary," http://www.airtransportaux.com/history.html, 13.

4. Genovese, *We Flew without Guns*, 96–97.

5. James Sallee Browne, General Record, Remarks by Commanding Officer, ATA Archives, London.

### 3. China in the Past

1. Coox, *Nomonhan*, 90–91.

2. Ford, *Flying Tigers*, 249.

3. Chennault, *Role of Defensive Pursuit*, 21–35.

4. Lawson, *The Long March*, 51–52.

5. Leonard, *I Flew for China*, 109.

### 4. The Long Road to China

1. Oldenburg Journal, Pan Am Collection, Richter Library, University of Miami, Coral Gables.

### 5. China National Aviation Corporation

1. Leary, *The Dragon's Wings*, 13–18.

2. Willett, *An Airline at War*, 76.

3. "Wife and 2 Children Die," *New York Times*, January 20, 1934, cnac.org /grooch01.htm/.

4. Banning, *Airlines of Pan Am since 1927*, 361.

5. Leonard, *I Flew for China*, 192.

6. Coox, *Nomonhan*, 993–94.

7. Crouch, *China's Wings*, 241.

8. Crouch, *China's Wings*, 290.

9. Crouch, *China's Wings*, 258.

### 6. The Flight

1. Genovese, *We Flew without Guns*, 159–62.

### 7. The Hump

1. Leary, *The Dragon's Wings*, 138–39.

2. Bond, *Wings for an Embattled China*, 273–75.

3. Tunner, *Over the Hump*, 58.

4. Tunner, *Over the Hump*, 18–19.

5. Goutiere, *Himalayan Rogue*, 78.

6. Rosbert, *Flying Tiger Joe's Adventure Story Cookbook*, 111–25.

7. Hanks, *Saga of CNAC #53*, 119.

8. McDonald and Evenson, *The Shadow Tiger*, 252–53.

9. McDonald and Evenson, *The Shadow Tiger*, 248–56; Hanks, *Saga of CNAC #53*, 114–29.

### 8. The Crew

1. Ford, *Flying Tigers*, 59.

2. Chennault, Record of Aerial Victories, no date, Chennault Collection, Hoover Institution on War, Revolution and Peace, Stanford University, Stanford, California.

3. "Capt. John J. Dean," Find a Grave, https://www.findagrave.com/memorial /92535998/john-j-dean.

### 9. The American Volunteer Group

1. Rosbert, *Flying Tiger Joe's Adventure Story Cookbook*, 43.

2. Ford, *Flying Tigers*, 74

3. Thomas G. Trumble, *History of the AVG*, July 4, 1942, Chennault Collection, Box 7, Folder 7, Hoover Institution.

4. Letter to CAMCO from Chennault, dated July 25, 1942, Flying Tiger Collection, Hoover Institution; Ford, *Flying Tigers*, 387–97.

### 10. The Plane

1. Davis, *The C-47 Skytrain in Action*, 32.

2. Goutiere, *Himalayan Rogue*, 86.

3. Douglas Aircraft Records, *Production History of C-47*, https://rzjets.net /aircraft/?page=20&typeid=275, 335.

## 11. The Search Takes Shape

1. Robertson, "George Robertson Remembers," 326.

## 12. China National Aviation Corporation Association

1. Crouch, *China's Wings*, 274.
2. Goutiere, *Himalayan Rogue*, 76.

## 13. MIA Recoveries, Inc.

1. Quinn, *Aluminum Trail*.

## 15. Planning Begins

1. Quinn, *The Aluminum Trail*, 7.

## 17. The Ascent

1. "C-47DL #41-18556 a.k.a. CNAC #60," http://www.miarecoveries.org/reports.

## 18. Enter JPAC

1. U.S. Department of Defense POW/MIA Accounting Agency, "Vision, Mission, Values."
2. U.S. Senate, Subcommittee on Financial and Contracting Oversight, "Mismanagement of POW/MIA Accounting."

## 21. The Next Step

1. PR Newswire, "Wreckage of a Hump Transport Plane," *Xinhua News Agency*, August 15, 2015, website discontinued.

## 22. Disappointment

1. Matthew M. Burke, "'So Many Questions': Botched Recovery Mission Didn't Follow JPAC's Own Protocol," *Stars and Stripes*, March 6, 2014, https://www.stripes.com/so-many-questions-botched-recovery-mission-didn-t-follow-jpac-s-own-protocol-1.271273.
2. "C-47B #43-48308," www.MIARecoveries.org/reports/.
3. Pacific Wrecks, "CV-240-7 Serial Number 82," February 6, 2019, https://pacificwrecks.com/aircraft/cv-240/AP-AEG.html.
4. "WWII Wreckage Found in Tripura," *Telegraph* (Calcutta), January 15, 2012, https://www.telegraphindia.com/1120115/jsp/frontpage/story_15007650.jsp.
5. "Debris of WWII US Aircraft Found in Tripura," *Zee News*, January 14, 2012, http://zeenews.india.com/news/nation/debris-of-ww-ii-us-aircraft-found-in-tripura_752599.html.

## Conclusion

1. U.S. Department of Defense, Prisoner of War/Missing Personnel Office, "Missing WWII Airman Identified," news release, April 21, 2011, http://www.dpaa.mil/portals/85/Documents/PressRelease/Archive/release_sims.pdf.
2. "Introduction of Shenzhen Longyue Charity Foundation," a paper distributed at our Chengdu meeting with Sun Chunlong.

## Epilogue

1. Ford, *Remains*, 225.

# Bibliography

Banning, Gene. *Airlines of Pan Am since 1927*. McLean VA: Paladwr Press, 2001.

Bond, W. Langhorne. *Wings for an Embattled China*. Bethlehem PA: Lehigh University Press, 2001.

Chennault, Claire. *The Role of Defensive Pursuit*. N.p.: n.p., 1933.

Coox, Alvin D. *Nomonhan*. Stanford CA: Stanford University Press, 1985.

Crouch, Gregory. *China's Wings*. New York: Bantam Books, 2012.

Davis. Larry. *C-47 Skytrain in Action*. Los Angeles: Squadron/Signal Publications, 1999.

Diebold, William. *Hell Is So Green*. Guilford CT: Lyons Press, 2012.

Ford, Daniel. *Flying Tigers*. Washington DC: Smithsonian Institution Press, 1991.

———. *Remains*. New York: Authors Choice Press, 2000.

Genovese, J. Gen. *We Flew without Guns*. Philadelphia: John C. Winston, 1945.

Goutiere, Peter. *Himalayan Rogue*. Paducah KY: Turner, 1994.

Gradidge, Jennifer. *DC-1, DC-2, DC-3: The First Seventy Years*. Tonbridge, England: Air Britain Historian, 2006.

Hanks, Fletcher. *Saga of CNAC #53*. Bloomington IN: Author House, 2004.

"Hump Transport Plane That Crashed in Tibet." PR News Wire, August 13, 2015. Website discontinued.

Lawson, Don. *The Long March*. New York: Thomas Y. Crowell, 1983.

Leary, William, Jr. *The Dragon's Wings*. Athens: University of Georgia Press, 1976.

Leonard, Royal. *I Flew for China*. New York: Doubleday, Doran, 1942.

Martin, Barry. *Forgotten Aviator: The Adventures of Royal Leonard*. Indianapolis IN: Self-published, 2011.

McDonald, William C., III, and Barbara Evenson. *The Shadow Tiger*. Birmingham AL: Self-published, 2016.

Oldenburg, Alfred V. "Nine of Us Flew from Miami to Calcutta." *CNAC Cannon Ball*, October 7, 1942. http://cnac.org/oldenburg01.htm.

Quinn, Chick Marrs. *The Aluminum Trail: How and Where They Died*. Lake City FL: Hunter Printing, 1989.

Robertson, George. "George Robertson Remembers." CNAC *Cannon Ball*, May 15, 2004. https://cnac.org/cannonball_2004_may.pdf.

Rosbert, Camille Joseph. *Flying Tiger Joe's Adventure Cookbook*. Franklin NC: Grant Poplar Press, 1985.

Stark, Jack. "Wings for Flying Cadets," *Miami Herald*, March 3, 1940.

Tunner, William H. *Over the Hump*. New York: Duell, Sloan, Pearce, 1964.

U.S. Department of Defense. DEFENSE POW/MIA Accounting Agency. "Vision, Mission, Values." N.d. https://www.dpaa.mil/About/Vision-Mission-Values/.

U.S. Senate, Subcommittee on Financial and Contracting Oversight. "Mismanagement of POW/MIA Accounting." Hearing before the Subcommittee on Financial and Contracting Oversight of the Committee on Homeland Security and Governmental Affairs. 113th Congress, 1st Session. August 1, 2013. https://www.gpo.gov/fdsys/pkg/chrg-113shrg82747/pdf/chrg-113shrg82747.pdf.

Willett, Robert L. *An Airline at War*. New York: Book Surge, 2010.

# Index

Italicized figure numbers refer to illustrations following page 74.

Carroll, Glen, 63–64
Central Aircraft Manufacturing Company (CAMCO), 76
Central Air Transport Company (CATC), 39, 74, 99
Chen, Angie, *fig. 28*; CNAC memorialization efforts, 148–49, 159, 185; connection to Colonel Liu of PLA, 147; connection to Hao Chen, 157–58; connection to Liu Xiatong, *fig. 12*, 54–55; hosts author on China trip, 186–90
Chen, Hao: at AVG reunion, 172; CNAC research project, 130–31, 157–58, 166, 169; and DPAA challenges, 178–81, 184
Chen, Hugh, 38
Chennault, Claire, 22, 33, 39, 40, 71, 72, 75, 77
Chiang, Madame, 22, 23, 38, 40–41
Chiang Kai-shek, 21–24, 31, 32, 38
Chin, Moon Fun, 38, 39, 44, 74, 92, 98–99, 103, 111, 112, 115, 190
China: celebration of seventieth anniversary of end of World War II, *figs. 19–21*, 144, 145, 149–50, 188; conflict with Japan, 19–20, 21, 23, 24–25, 35, 36–45; involvement in MIA searches, 135, 141–44, 146, 148, 161–63, 165–70, 178–81; rise of Communism in, 22–23, 31, 35; transportation modernization, 31–32. *See also* CNAC
*China's Wings* (Crouch), 101
Chinese Air Force: Chennault's leadership, 22, 40; combat with Japan, 24, 36, 65; seizure of CNAC plans and operations, 36–38; and status of AVG, 72
Chinese National Party, 21
Chou En-lai, 23
Chungking, 25, 32, 35, 36, 40
Civil Aviation Museum, 148–49, 158, 159
Clark, Arthur, 117–18, 121, 125
Clipper Ships, Pan Am, 35, 36, 43
CNAC (China National Aviation Corporation), *fig. 5*; aircraft models, 79–85, 100–101; books and research on, 90–92, 101; Chinese crew members, 51, 73–74; early route development, 32–35; establishment of Hump crossings, 42, 45, 57–58; involvement in Sino-Japanese conflict, 24, 35, 36–45; Japanese attacks on aircraft of, 41, 65–66, 80, 81, 108; Jimmie Browne recruited to, 26–27; reunions, 92–94; Second Generation, 185, 187, 188
CNAC Association, *fig. 13*, 98, 110–16, 122–23, 124
CNAC No. 60, *fig. 10*, *fig. 18*, 82–84, 85, 103
CNAC.org, 91–92
Cohn, Christine, 135
Coldren, Russell, 104
Cole, Helen (cousin of Jimmie Browne), 5, 11

Colon, Dan, 179–80
Communist Party, 22–23, 31
Cook, Charles, 63
Coulson, Bert, 98
Coulson, Eve, 98, 110
Crouch, Gregory, 45, 101
Curtiss-Wright, 32, 33

Dali Mountain. *See* Cangshan Mountain
Davis, Larry, 83
DC-2 (aircraft model), 41, 79–81
DC-3 (aircraft model), 39–40, 41, 79, 81–82, 83
Dean, Bess (Klein), 68, 70
Dean, John Joseph, *fig. 8*; aviation career, 68–73, 78, 114, 119–20; events of last flight, 49–54; production of documentary on, 157–58
Dean, Robert, 68
Dean, Roy, 68, 69, 70, 157
DeKantzow, Peter, 111
DeKantzow, Syd, 39, 57
Department of Veterans Affairs, 160, 170
Dinjan, 42, 45, 49, 57
Disabled American Veterans, 123
Distinguished Flying Cross eligibility, 171
Donald, W. H., 40
Doolittle, Jimmy, 99
DPAA (Defense POW/MIA Accounting Agency): involvement in Jimmie Browne search, 137, 143–44, 145–46, 158–65, 167, 168, 178–81; mission of, 132, 192–93; privatization prospects, 107–8; Tilley's criticism of, 173–74. *See also* JPAC
DPMO (Defense POW/Missing Personnel Office), 133–36
DST (Douglas Sleeper Transport), 83
Duan Haihong, 153

Eddy, M. F., 9
Eisenhower, Dwight D., 79
embassy, Chinese: author's first contact with, 142; author's meeting with, 161, 165–66; cooperation with Jimmie Browne search, 166–70, 172; invites author to Beijing, 145; involvement in PLA, 146–47; search efforts ended, 181
Eurasia Aviation Corporation, 32, 39, 81

Fan Jianchuan, *fig. 26*, 159–60, 187, 188
Feeney, Tom, 134
Ferry Command, 4, 59
First Sino-Japanese War (1894–95), 20
*Flying the Hump* (Liu), 54–55, 111–12, 119
Flying Tigers (American Volunteer Group), xiii, 27, 40, 44, 50, 69–72, 75–78
Ford, Daniel, 22, 77, 195
Fox, Jim, 60–61, 67, 112, 122–23